T0077019

ONLY JESUS

WHAT IT REALLY MEANS TO BE SAVED

From the bestselling author of *The Gospel According to Jesus*

JOHN MACARTHUR

THOMAS NELSON
Since 1798

Only Jesus: What It Really Means to Be Saved

Copyright © 1988. 1993, 2008 by John F. MacArthur Jr.
Derived from material previously published in *The Gospel According to Jesus*.
Abridgment by Phillip R. Johnson.

Published in Nashville, Tennessee, by Thomas Nelson. Thomas Nelson is a
registered trademark of HarperCollins Christian Publishing, Inc.

Published in association with the literary agency of Wolgemuth &
Associates, Inc.

Thomas Nelson titles may be purchased in bulk for educational, business,
fund-raising, or sales promotional use. For information, please e-mail
SpecialMarkets@ThomasNelson.com.

All Scripture quotations in this book, except those noted otherwise, are from
the *New American Standard Bible*®. Copyright ©1960, 1962, 1963, 1968,
1971, 1972, 1973, 1975, 1977, 1988, and 1995 by The Lockman Foundation.
Used by permission.

Scripture quotations marked KJV are from the King James Version. Public
domain.

Wherever words are italicized in Scripture quotations, the italics have been
added for emphasis.

ISBN 978-0-7852-3075-5 (hardcover)
ISBN 978-0-3101-0825-2 (ebook)

Cover design: Jamie DeBruyn
Interior design: Emily Ghattas

Printed in the United States of America

20 21 22 23 24 25 26 27 28 / LSC / 10 9 8 7 6 5 4 3

Contents

Introduction

COME AND DIE

What did Jesus mean when He said, "Follow Me"? He certainly wasn't calling anyone to a life of ease and earthly prosperity.

In the plainest possible terms He frequently made clear that His call to discipleship was a call to self-denial, crucifixion, and daily death (cf. Luke 9:23). Following Him meant dying to self, hating one's own life in this world, and serving Him (John 12:24–26).

In Luke 14:26–27, He said, "If anyone comes to Me, and does not hate his own father and mother and wife and children and brothers and sisters, yes, and even his own life, he cannot be My disciple. Whoever does not carry his own cross and come after Me cannot be My disciple."

Difficult demands? *Impossible* in human terms. Yet those are Jesus' exact words—unequivocal, unadorned, unmitigated by any explanation or soothing rationalization.

He was sounding a note that is missing from much that passes for evangelism today. His "follow Me" was a call to surrender to His lordship.

"[We preach] Christ Jesus as *Lord*," the apostle Paul wrote (2 Cor. 4:5). "Jesus is Lord" was the core of the early church's confession of faith, the primary nucleus of truth affirmed by every true Christian (1 Cor. 12:3). What must we do to be saved? "Believe in the *Lord* Jesus, and you will be saved" (Acts 16:31). "If you confess with your mouth *Jesus as Lord*, and believe in your heart that God raised Him from the dead, you will be saved" (Rom. 10:9). The lordship of Christ is clearly at the heart of true saving faith.

True salvation produces a heart that voluntarily responds to the ever-awakening reality of Christ's lordship. Because we are sinful creatures, we can never respond as obediently as we should. We experience pathetic failures or extended periods of spiritual dullness. But if we are true believers, we will not fall back into the cold, hardhearted, determined unbelief and rebellion of our former state. Those who live like that have no reason to think they have ever been redeemed.

The gospel is a call to faith—and genuine faith demands our surrender to Jesus as Lord. Those who would come to Him for salvation must be willing to acquiesce to His sovereign authority. No one who rejects His right to rule can lay claim to Him as Savior. Our Lord had no interest in gathering half-hearted or occasional followers. His hard demands are therefore stressed repeatedly in Scripture. That's one of several reasons the gospel message is a stumbling block to some and folly to others (1 Cor. 1:23).

But there is a great deal of confusion nowadays regarding the gospel message. The visible church is full of people who want to soften Jesus' message, remove the stumbling blocks, and make the message sound sophisticated. There is no legitimate way to achieve those goals, and those who try invariably truncate, twist, or trash the biblical message.

Believers must look to Jesus—*only* Jesus—as the starting point, the proper focus, and the anchor of gospel truth. Following Him doesn't mean adding Him as an adjunct to a list of things we already love and serve. Radical changes are wrought in the hearts and lives of those who truly answer Christ's call to discipleship. "He is Lord of all" (Acts 10:36), and genuine believers will confess and yield to that truth. Those who treat Him merely as an addendum to their other pastimes and priorities have not yet truly believed in Him.

This book examines the gospel as Christ himself proclaimed it—with an eye toward gaining a thorough and proper understanding of the true way of salvation. He is, after all, the one true "author and perfecter of faith" (Heb. 12:2). He is the One (ultimately the *only* One) to whom we must turn for words of eternal life (John 6:68).

Let's explore what He had to say about the gospel.

CHAPTER 1

Master and Slaves

"Jesus is Lord" (1 Cor. 12:3).

That is the fundamental article of faith for all true Christians. It's the first essential confession of faith every true Christian must make: "If you confess with your mouth Jesus as Lord, and believe in your heart that God raised Him from the dead, you will be saved" (Rom. 10:9). You cannot remove the lordship of Christ from the gospel message without undermining faith at its core.

Jesus' own teaching and ministry always kept the issue of His lordship at the center. He never once shied away from declaring His authority as sovereign Master. He proclaimed it to disciples, to enemies, and to casual inquirers alike—refusing to tone down the implications of His demand for unconditional surrender. When Jesus called people to follow Him, He was not seeking companions to be His sidekicks or admirers whom He could entertain with miracles. He was calling people to yield completely and unreservedly to His lordship.

A Word about Words

The expression most often translated "Lord" in the English New Testament is the Greek word *kurios*. It speaks of someone who has power, ownership, and an unquestionable right to command. A nearly synonymous Greek term also sometimes translated "Lord" in the New Testament is *despotes*. That word (the root of our English word *despot*) describes a ruler with absolute power over his subjects.

Both words are used in reference to Christ as Lord in the New Testament. In John 13:13, for instance, Jesus took the title *kurios* for Himself: "You call Me Teacher and Lord [*kurios*]; and you are right, for so I am." Jude 4 employs both words in parallel fashion: "Ungodly persons . . . turn the grace of our God into licentiousness and deny our only Master [*despotes*] and Lord [*kurios*], Jesus Christ."

Both words belonged to the vocabulary of slavery in New Testament times. They describe a master who has absolute dominion over someone whom he literally owns. His subjects are duty-bound to obey their lord—not merely because they choose to do so but because they have no rightful liberty to do otherwise. Wherever there was a lord (*kurios*) or a master (*despotes*), there was always a slave (*doulos*). One idea is essential to explain the other. That explains Jesus' incredulity at the practice of those who paid homage to Him with their lips but not with their lives: "Why do you call Me, 'Lord, Lord,' and do not do what I say?" (Luke 6:46).

That Greek word *doulos* is used in Scripture to describe what it means to be a true Christian: "He who was called while free, is Christ's slave [*doulos*]. You were bought with a price" (1 Cor. 7:22–23).

Doulos is not an ambiguous term. It suggests a very specific concept, which—while repugnant to our culture and our natural minds—should not be toned down or backed away from. It is the main Greek word that was used to describe the lowest abject bondslave—a person who was literally owned by a master who could legally force him to work without wages. In other words, a *doulos* was a person without standing or rights.

English Bibles tend to shield us from the full force of the word *doulos* because of an ages-old tendency among Bible translators to tone down the literal sense of the word—translating it as "servant," or "bond servant" rather than "slave."

But service and slavery are not really the same thing. A slave is someone who lacks personal freedom and personal rights—whose very existence is defined by service to another. This is total, unqualified submission to the control and the directives of a higher authority—*slavery*, not merely service at one's own discretion.

For example, in Matthew 6:24, Jesus said, "No one can be a slave to two masters" (literal translation). That rendering is much stronger (and actually makes better sense) than what you will find in most versions: "No one can serve two masters." An employee with two jobs could indeed *serve* two masters. But slavery—not merely service—is what the word *doulos* and all its derivatives speak of.

The distinctive idea is ownership. We are

not our own, for we have been bought with a price (1 Cor. 6:19–20). We have a Master who purchased us (2 Peter 2:1). To be specific, we were purchased for God with the precious blood of Christ (Rev. 5:9). This is the very essence of what it means to be a Christian: "For not one of us lives for himself, and not one dies for himself; for if we live, we live for the Lord, or if we die, we die for the Lord; therefore whether we live or die, we are the Lord's. For to this end Christ died and lived again, that He might be Lord both of the dead and of the living" (Rom. 14:7–9).

Why Such a Revolting Concept?

In one sense, we can understand why Bible translators have tended to soften the implications of *doulos*. The word *slavery* conjures up so much negative imagery and so many strong passions that we instinctively shy away from it.

That's not a modern development. Slavery was by no means a glamorous institution in first-century culture either. It was a fixture in Roman societies—perfectly legal, pervasive, and rarely challenged. Not all slaves were mistreated, but many were, and Roman-style slavery was notorious for its inability to curtail the terrible abuses that *did* occur. Slaves themselves, of course, had absolutely no control over whether they were well treated or oppressed. So even though slavery was widely regarded as a necessary component of the social and economic structure, the idea of *being* a slave was universally loathsome. No one wanted to be anyone's *doulos*.

In that regard, Jesus' portrayal of discipleship as slavery had no more appeal to the popular tastes or felt needs of His time than it does today. In fact, because most people in Jesus' time were so familiar with real-life slavery, they had a much more vivid mental picture than we do of what Jesus was demanding when He called for absolute self-denial and surrender to His lordship. He was certainly not trying to appeal to a longing for self-esteem or make discipleship look enticing to the people of Galilee and Judea when He spoke about the cost of following Him. They understood far better than we do what a menial position He was calling them to. In fact, many people in the early church *were* slaves. That is why there are so many passages in the Epistles giving instructions about how slaves were to behave in order to reflect the character and holiness of Christ (Eph. 6:5–8; Col. 3:22; 1 Tim. 6:1–2; Titus 2:9–10; 1 Peter 2:18–20).

The Problem with a Feel-Good Gospel

The idea of the Christian as a slave and Christ as Master is almost totally missing from the vocabulary of contemporary evangelical Christianity. Not only is *slave* a bad word loaded with political incorrectness, but our generation also loves the concepts of freedom and personal fulfillment. People crave autonomy, and as the church has become increasingly worldly, the biblical truth of our duty to Him as our absolute Lord and Master has all but disappeared from the evangelical consciousness. The church in our generation has reduced all of saving faith and Christian discipleship to a thoughtless (but more politically correct) cliché: "a personal relationship with Jesus." The ambiguity of the phrase reflects the destructive vagueness with which people have been handling (and mishandling) the gospel for the past several decades. As if Christ could be someone's intimate friend *without* being that person's Lord.

But as we shall shortly observe, His only true *friends* were those who did what He said (John 15:14).

Slavery to Christ is not a minor or secondary feature of true discipleship. This is not merely symbolic or illustrative language. It is exactly how Jesus Himself defined the "personal relationship" He must have with every true follower (John 12:26; 15:20). And that fact is stressed throughout the New Testament.

For example, the opening words of several New Testament epistles include their various authors' confessions that they were but slaves of Christ (Rom. 1:1; Phil. 1:1; Titus 1:1; James 1:1; 2 Peter 1:1; Jude 1; Rev. 1:1). Every true disciple in the apostolic church understood this truth completely, because if all the *apostles* confessed that they were Jesus' slaves, those under the apostles' oversight certainly had to be slaves of Christ as well.

As a matter of fact, the fundamental aspects of slavery are the very features of our redemption that Scripture puts the most stress on. We are *chosen* (Eph. 1:4–5; 1 Peter 1:1; 2:9); bought (1 Cor. 6:20; 7:23); *owned* by our Master (Rom. 14:7–9; 1 Cor. 6:19; Titus 2:14); *subject to the Master's will and control* over us (Acts 5:29; Rom.

6:16–19; Phil. 2:5–8); and *totally dependent* on the Master for everything in our lives (2 Cor. 9:8–11; Phil. 4:19). We will ultimately be *called to account* (Rom. 14:12); *evaluated* (2 Cor. 5:10); and *either chastened or rewarded* by Him (Heb. 12:5–11; 1 Cor. 3:14). Those are all essential components of slavery.

What Would Jesus Say?

Jesus Himself introduced the slave metaphor in the New Testament. He frequently drew a direct connection between slavery and discipleship. In Matthew 10:24, for example, he said, "A disciple is not above his teacher, nor a slave above his master." He demanded that His followers deny themselves completely. He instructed them to be ready to die for Him. He called for them to relinquish all their normal priorities—including family, friends, personal plans, ambitions, and everything else in this world. Their whole lives were explicitly and irrevocably placed under His authority. His lordship was total and nonnegotiable. Those were His terms, and would-be disciples who tried to dictate *different* terms were always turned away (Luke 9:59–62).

Not Mere Slaves, but Slaves Who Are Friends

Perhaps the key passage on Jesus' demand for implicit obedience is one we have already alluded to briefly—John 15:14–15: "You are My friends, if you do what I command you. No longer do I call you slaves, for the slave does not know what his master is doing; but I have called you friends, for all things that I have heard from My Father I have made known to you."

It is vital to understand that Jesus was not suggesting that obedience *makes* someone His friend—as if His favor could be earned through service. He was saying, however, that obedience is a singular proof that someone *is* His friend. Implicit obedience to His commandments is the necessary, expected, and natural fruit of genuine love for Him. It is also therefore the telltale mark of authentic saving faith. Again, a necessary inference is that someone who does not do what Jesus says is not a friend of His at all. He was describing as clearly as possible a master-slave relationship.

Look at the context. Jesus clearly explains why He makes a differentiation between mere slaves and friends: "The slave does not know what his master is doing." In other words, a slave's obedience is implicit, unhesitating; and he is not owed any explanation or rationale from the Master. He is to obey whether he understands why or not.

But Jesus had kept nothing secret from His disciples. His purposes were fully known to them: "all things that I have heard from My Father I have made known to you" (v. 15). They were therefore much more than mere slaves to Him. They were His friends as well, privy to His thoughts and purposes (cf. 1 Cor. 2:16). In a similar way, every ruler would have friends among his subjects to whom he might reveal personal matters, but they were still his subjects.

Friendship with one's lord or master does not nullify the authority inherent in the relationship. He was still their Lord, and they were still His *douloi*. In other words, as friends, they were not His "buddies" in the sense of being casual chums or peers with Him in the relationship. He remained their Lord and Master, and they belonged completely to Him. In other words, Jesus' disciples—though friends, totally devoted to their Master in love—are still slaves, marked by their obedience.

Slavery and True Liberty

Understood correctly, then, the gospel is an invitation to slavery. When we call people to faith in Christ, we need to stress that fact in the same way Jesus did. On the one hand, the gospel is a proclamation of freedom to sin's captives and liberty to people who are broken by the bondage of sin's power over them. On the other hand, it is a summons to a whole different kind of slavery: "Having been freed from sin, you became slaves of righteousness" (Rom. 6:18). As the apostle Peter wrote, "Act as free men, and do not use your freedom as a covering for evil, but use it as bondslaves of God" (1 Peter 2:16).

Both sides of the equation are vital. There is a glorious freedom in being the slaves of Christ, because "if the Son makes you free, you will be free indeed" (John 8:36). On the other hand, being a true follower of Christ means the end of human autonomy.

No message can rightly be called the gospel if it glosses over or denies those truths. Jesus Himself called sinners to give up their independence, deny themselves, submit to an alien will, and abandon all rights in order to be owned and

20

controlled by the Lord. By confessing Jesus as Lord (*kurios*), we automatically confess that we are His slaves (*douloi*).

There is also no legitimate way to adjust Jesus' message to make it sound appealing to people who admire Him but are not prepared to obey Him.

As we work our way through some of the most important chapters of Jesus' life, ministry, and public discourses, you will see that He consistently made His lordship a prominent theme. It is the unifying idea in the story of redemption, the song of the redeemed, and the reason for the gospel in the first place, "that at the name of Jesus every knee will bow, of those who are in heaven and on earth and under the earth, and that every tongue will confess that Jesus Christ is Lord, to the glory of God the Father" (Phil. 2:10–11).

CHAPTER 2

What Is the
Gospel Message?

Ask the typical Christian today to summarize the gospel, and you will invariably hear phrases like, "accept Jesus Christ as your personal Savior"; "ask Jesus into your heart"; "invite Christ into your life"; or "make a decision for Christ." Christians have become so accustomed to using those expressions that it might surprise you to learn none of them are based on biblical terminology. They are products of a diluted gospel.

Jesus taught that the cost of following Him is high, that the way is narrow and few find it

(Matt. 7:13–14). He said many who call Him Lord will be forbidden from entering the kingdom of heaven.

He gave this sobering warning: "Not everyone who says to Me, 'Lord, Lord,' will enter the kingdom of heaven; *but he who does the will of My Father who is in heaven will enter*. Many will say to Me on that day, 'Lord, Lord, did we not prophesy in Your name, and in Your name cast out demons, and in Your name perform many miracles?' And then I will declare to them, 'I never knew you; depart from Me, *you who practice lawlessness*'" (Matt. 7:21–23).

He was not speaking about an isolated group of fringe followers. There will be "many" on that day who will stand before Him, stunned to learn they are not included in the kingdom.

Countless churchgoers today believe that because they recited a prayer, signed on a dotted line, walked an aisle, or had some other experience, they are saved and should never question their salvation. But Scripture encourages us to examine ourselves to determine if we are in the faith (2 Cor. 13:5). Peter wrote, "Be all the more diligent to make certain about His calling and choosing you" (2 Peter 1:10). It is right to examine our lives and evaluate the fruit we bear, for "each tree is known by its own fruit" (Luke 6:44).

The Bible teaches clearly that the evidence of God's work in a life is the inevitable fruit of transformed behavior (1 John 3:10). Faith that does not result in righteous living is dead and cannot save (James 2:14–17). Professing Christians utterly lacking the fruit of true righteousness will find no biblical basis for assurance of salvation (1 John 2:4).

Real salvation is not only justification. It cannot be isolated from regeneration, sanctification, and ultimately glorification. Salvation is the work of God through which we are "conformed to the image of His Son" (Rom. 8:29). Genuine assurance comes from seeing the Holy Spirit's transforming work in one's life, not from clinging to the memory of some experience.

Savior *and* Lord

Much confusion about the gospel nowadays stems from the tendency to separate the fact that Jesus is sovereign Lord from the truth that he is a merciful Savior. Those are not contradictions to be pitted against one another. Jesus is both Savior and Lord (Luke 2:11), and no true believer would ever dispute that. "Savior" and "Lord" are separate offices, but we must be careful not to partition them in such a way that we divide Christ (cf. 1 Cor. 1:13).

The two clearest statements on the way of salvation in all of Scripture both emphasize Jesus' lordship: "Believe in the *Lord* Jesus, and you will be saved" (Acts 16:31); and "If you confess with your mouth *Jesus as Lord*, and believe in your heart that God raised Him from the dead, you will be saved" (Rom. 10:9). Peter's sermon at Pentecost concluded with this declaration: "Let all the house of Israel know for certain that God has made Him *both Lord and Christ*—this Jesus whom you crucified" (Acts 2:36). No promise of salvation is ever extended to those who refuse to accede to Christ's lordship.

True faith is not lip service. Our Lord Himself pronounced condemnation on those who worshiped Him with their lips but not with their lives (Matt. 15:7–9). He does not become anyone's Savior until that person receives Him for who He is—Lord of all (Acts 10:36). To spurn his lordship while claiming to trust Him as Savior is to live a lie.

By Grace through Faith

Salvation is solely by grace through faith (Eph. 2:8). That is the heart and soul of the gospel message. But it means nothing if we begin with a misunderstanding of *grace* or a faulty definition of *faith*.

God's grace is not a static attribute whereby He passively accepts hardened, unrepentant sinners. Grace does not change a person's standing before God yet leave his character untouched. Real grace is not license to do whatever we choose. True grace, according to Scripture, teaches us "to deny ungodliness and worldly desires and to live sensibly, righteously and godly in the present age" (Titus 2:12). Grace is the power of God to fulfill our new covenant duties, however inconsistently we obey at times. Clearly, grace does not grant permission to live in the flesh; it supplies power to live in the Spirit.

Faith, like grace, is not static. Saving faith is inseparable from repentance, surrender, and a supernatural longing to obey. None of those responses can be classified exclusively as a human work, any more than believing itself is solely a human effort.

Repentance is always at the core of genuine saving faith. Repentance involves a recognition of one's utter sinfulness and a turning from self and sin to God (cf. 1 Thess. 1:9). Repentance is not a human work; it is the inevitable result of *God's* work in a human heart.

The result, of course, is radical change of direction—a true spiritual conversion. Both the defiant sinner's rebellion and the careless sinner's indifference are overcome by the work of God's grace (Titus 2:11–12).

God's grace eliminates boasting (Rom. 3:27) and self-righteousness (Phil. 3:9), but it does not eliminate works per se. It does away with works that are the result of human effort alone (Eph. 2:8). It abolishes any attempt to merit God's favor by our works (v. 9). But it does not deter God's foreordained purpose that our walk should be characterized by good works. Works are the fruit, not the root, of a sinner's salvation.

We must remember above all that salvation is a sovereign work of God. Biblically it is defined by what it produces, not by what one does to get it. "We are His workmanship, created in Christ Jesus for good works, which God prepared beforehand so that we would walk in them" (Eph. 2:10). As a part of His saving work,

God will produce repentance, faith, sanctification, yieldedness, obedience, and ultimately glorification. Since He is not dependent on human effort in producing those elements, an experience that lacks any of them cannot be the saving work of God.

Those who are truly born of God have a faith that cannot fail to overcome the world (1 John 5:4). We may sin (1 John 2:1)—we *will* sin—but the process of sanctification can never stall completely. God is at work in us (Phil. 2:13), and He will continue to perfect us until the day of Christ (Phil. 1:6; 1 Thess. 5:23–24).

CHAPTER 3

You Must Be Born Again

Not everyone who claims to be a Christian really is. Unbelievers *do* make false professions of faith in Christ, and people who are not truly Christians can be deceived into thinking they are.

Jesus said He came "to seek and to save that which was lost" (Luke 19:10). But in his dealings with sinners, He never encouraged a quick, easy, or shallow response. He turned away far more prospects than He won, refusing to proclaim a message that would give anyone false hope.

Jesus' meeting with Nicodemus in John 3

is an example of this. It is the earliest of His one-on-one evangelistic encounters recorded in the Gospels. It's ironic that Jesus, who so often confronted the Pharisees' unbelief and outright antagonism, began His evangelistic ministry by answering a leading Pharisee who approached Him. We might expect Jesus to welcome Nicodemus warmly, but Jesus knew the unbelief and self-righteousness of Nicodemus's heart.

Nicodemus begins the conversation with this confession of faith: "Rabbi, we know that you have come from God as a teacher; for no one can do these signs that You do unless God is with him" (John 3:2). He was intrigued with Christ. There had not been a prophet for four hundred years.

Jesus, who "knew all men" (John 2:24), understood what was really on Nicodemus's heart. He ignored Nicodemus's profession of faith and instead answered a question Nicodemus didn't even ask: "Truly, truly, I say to you, unless one is born again he cannot see the kingdom of God" (John 3:3).

Nicodemus was clearly stunned by Jesus' answer. It included four critical truths that must have astonished him.

The Futility of Religion

Nicodemus was "a ruler of the Jews" (John 3:1), a member of the Sanhedrin, the highest ruling body of the Jewish nation. Perhaps he came by night because he didn't want the whole world to see him and think he was representing all the Sanhedrin. Or maybe he was afraid of what the other Pharisees would think. They were known to put people out of the synagogue for believing in Jesus (John 9:22). Nevertheless, he came— unlike his colleagues—with a sincere desire to learn.

The Pharisees were hyper-legalists who externalized religion. Although they were deeply religious, they were no nearer the kingdom of God than a prostitute. Their credo included fastidious adherence to more than six hundred laws, many of which were simply their own inventions. They seemed to believe their severe, burdensome rules and rigorous codes of conduct made them holier than if they simply followed Scripture alone. Nicodemus may have expected Christ to commend him for his strict legalism. Instead, Jesus confronted him with the futility of his religion: "You must be born again" (John 3:7).

Nicodemus's reply has often been misunderstood: "How can a man be born when he is old? He cannot enter a second time into his mother's womb and be born, can he?" (John 3:4). Nicodemus was not speaking in literal terms. We must give him credit for a little common sense. A teacher himself, Nicodemus understood the rabbinical method of using figurative language to teach spiritual truth, and he was merely picking up Jesus' symbolism. He was really saying, "I *can't* start all over. It's too late. I've gone too far in my religious system to start over. There's no hope for me if I must begin from the beginning."

Jesus was demanding that Nicodemus forsake everything he stood for, and Nicodemus knew it. Christ was challenging him with the most difficult demand He could make. Nicodemus would gladly have given money, fasted, or performed any ritual Jesus could have prescribed. But to call him to a spiritual rebirth was asking him to acknowledge his own insufficiency and to turn away from everything he was committed to.

Nicodemus got the message, and it's clear that he was staggered by it. He asked Jesus, "How can these things be?" (v. 9).

The Unity of Revelation

"Jesus answered and said to him, 'Are you the teacher of Israel and do not understand these things?'" (v. 10). That rebuke from the Lord completely silenced Nicodemus. If Nicodemus said any more, John does not record it. The silence is understandable. Jesus' challenge of Nicodemus's aptitude as a spiritual teacher was a devastating putdown.

Jesus' comeback also made an important doctrinal point. The clear implication is that the Old Testament plainly taught the way of salvation (cf. 2 Tim. 3:15). Jesus was not announcing a new or distinct means of redemption (cf. Matt. 5:17). Even in the Old Testament, eternal life was never a payoff for those who observed the law; it was a gift to those who humbly and by faith sought redemption from their sin. Yet it always meant a new start, a rebirth, a turning from sin to God. Nicodemus, as a teacher of the law, should have understood that. He should have been familiar with the words of the Lord recorded by Isaiah:

> "Wash yourselves, make yourselves clean;
> Remove the evil of your deeds from My
> sight.

Cease to do evil,
Learn to do good . . . .
Come now, and let us reason together,"
Says the LORD,
"Though your sins are as scarlet,
They will be as white as snow;
Though they are red like crimson,
They will be like wool."

ISAIAH 1:16–18

The central theme of the Old Testament is redemption by grace. But incredibly, the Pharisees entirely missed it. In their rigid emphasis on religious works, they deemphasized the truth of God's grace and forgiveness to sinners—a theme that runs through the Old Testament. They stressed obedience to law, not conversion to the Lord, as the way to gain eternal life.

They were so determined to earn a righteousness of their own (Rom. 10:3) that they neglected the marvelous truth of Habakkuk 2:4: "The righteous will live by his faith." They looked to Abraham as their father but overlooked the key lesson of his life: "He believed in the LORD; and [the LORD] reckoned it to him as righteousness" (Gen. 15:6). They scoured the psalms for laws they could add to their list, but they ignored the most sublime truth of all—that God forgives sins, covers transgressions, and refuses to impute iniquity to sinners who turn to Him (Ps. 32:1–2). They anticipated the coming of their Messiah but closed their eyes to the fact that He would come to die as a sacrifice for sin (Isa. 53:4–9). They were confident that they were guides to the blind, lights to those in darkness, correctors of the foolish, and teachers of the immature (cf. Rom. 2:19–20), but they missed the most basic lesson of God's law: that they themselves were sinners in need of redemption.

People have always stumbled at the simplicity of salvation. That is why there are so many cults. Each one has a unique slant on the doctrine of salvation—and each one corrupts the simplicity of the gospel revealed in God's Word (cf. 2 Cor. 11:3) by espousing salvation by human works. Each one of the major cults claims to have a key that unlocks the secret of salvation, yet they are all alike in propagating self-righteous achievement as the way to God.

From start to finish, God's Word disproves them all, and in a wonderfully consistent way. Its message, woven through sixty-six books, written over a span of fifteen hundred years by more than forty different authors, is marvelously unified and congruous. The message is simply that God graciously saves repentant sinners who come to Him in faith. There is no secret there, no mystery, no obscurity, and no complexity. If Nicodemus had truly understood God's Word, he would have known that much.

The Necessity of Regeneration

Despite his great ability as a teacher and his obsession with the details of the law, Nicodemus had fallen short. Jesus did not try to mask or soften that fact. Nicodemus was nurturing a great sin he was not even aware of—the sin of unbelief. When Nicodemus said, "I don't understand," what he really meant was, "I don't believe." Unbelief always begets ignorance.

Verses 11–12 confirm that unbelief was the real issue. There Jesus says, "Truly, truly, I say to you, we speak of what we know and testify of what we have seen, and you do not accept our testimony. If I told you earthly things and you do not believe, how will you believe if I tell you heavenly things?" Nicodemus claimed he didn't understand. Jesus wanted him to know that faith comes before full understanding. As Paul wrote in 1 Corinthians 2:14, "A natural man does not accept the things of the Spirit of God, for they are foolishness to him; and he cannot understand them, because they are spiritually appraised." Spiritual truth does not register in the mind of one who does not believe; unbelief understands nothing.

What a blow this was to Nicodemus's self-righteousness! He had come to Jesus with a smug profession of faith: "We know that you have come from God as a teacher" (John 3:2). In essence, Jesus responded, "No you don't. You don't understand Scripture. You don't know the basics about salvation. You don't even understand earthly things. What good would it do for Me to expound heavenly truth to you?"

Like most religious unbelievers, Nicodemus did not want to confess that he was a helpless sinner. Jesus knew the truth. Nicodemus thought of himself as a great spiritual leader. Jesus had reduced him to nothing.

"No one has ascended into heaven, but He who descended from heaven: the Son of Man" (John 3:13). With that statement of His divine origin, Jesus rebuked Nicodemus's shallow faith and destroyed his system of religion by works.

No one can ascend to heaven; that is, no one can earn his way there. God has come down from heaven and spoken to us by His Son (Heb. 1:1–2). We could never climb to heaven and find the answers for ourselves. The only Person who has that kind of access to God is the One who descended from heaven. He is not merely a teacher sent by God; He is in fact God in human flesh. We either accept what He says, or we are left with our sin.

This, then, is His message: "You must be born again" (John 3:7). Regeneration is no option, but rather an absolute necessity. No one—not even the most religious Pharisee—is exempt from the divine call to a new birth. And thus we have the starting point of all gospel truth: *salvation is impossible apart from divinely wrought regeneration.*

The Reality of Redemption

When Nicodemus offered no further response, Jesus lovingly and graciously explained to him the new birth in all its simplicity. Beginning in John 3:14, Jesus introduced the details of the way of salvation. He chose an Old Testament illustration of salvation, as if to underscore His rebuke to Nicodemus for not understanding the truth of Scripture: "As Moses lifted up the serpent in the wilderness, even so must the Son of Man be lifted up; so that whoever believes will in Him have eternal life" (vv. 14–15). Surely Nicodemus knew that story. Why hadn't he ever understood its truth?

Numbers 21 gives the full account of the serpent in the wilderness. The Israelites were wandering around, having left Egypt but having not yet entered the Promised Land. They had been complaining incessantly—grumbling about the food, muttering about Moses, and whining about how bad their condition was. Finally, when God had enough, He sent a plague in the form of hundreds of poisonous snakes. The snakes overran the camp, and the rebellious people were bitten. When they realized they were dying, they repented. They came to Moses, asking him to intercede on their behalf. God in His mercy forgave them and told Moses to construct a pole with a bronze serpent at the top. He was to erect it in the center of the camp. The Lord gave this promise: "Everyone who is bitten, when he looks at it, he will live" (Num. 21:8). He did not prescribe a ritual or a chant. Just so, salvation doesn't happen by religious ceremony. That was true when the Israelites were in the wilderness; it was true for Nicodemus; it is true today.

Jesus was not, however, painting a picture of easy faith. He was showing Nicodemus the necessity of repentance. In fact, Jesus used this particular illustration precisely because it challenged Nicodemus's Pharisaism. Nicodemus knew the story of the bronze serpent well. As a leader of the Jewish nation, no doubt he identified with Moses. Jesus was showing him instead that he must identify with the sinning, rebellious Israelites.

Nicodemus knew well the helpless state of the Israelites for whom the bronze serpent was erected. They were sinful, defiant rebels against God. They had been judged, and they were dying. They came to Moses in absolute shame and utter repentance, saying, "We have sinned, because we have spoken against the LORD and you" (Num. 21:7). Undoubtedly many were already sick and dying, fast losing their strength. They were in no position to glance flippantly at the pole and then proceed with lives of rebellion. It is noteworthy that Moses records no further occurrence of the kind of rebellion that had brought about their judgment. They turned to God in desperation and with genuine repentance. Jesus was demanding that Nicodemus do the same.

The issue was sin. Jesus was challenging this great teacher of the law to acknowledge that he had been bitten by the great serpent, Satan, and to come to the Lord for salvation. The very concept would have been repugnant to a Pharisee. It cut at the core of his self-righteousness. Far from giving Nicodemus an illustration of the ease of belief, our Lord established a painful condition for Nicodemus's salvation: he must acknowledge his sinfulness and repent. He must be willing to include himself among the sinful, snake-bitten, repentant Israelites.

The illustration of the bronze serpent also pictured Jesus' death as the price of redemption. Just as Moses lifted up that serpent, so the Son of Man would be lifted up on a pole—the cross of crucifixion. The word "must" in verse 14 is significant; Christ *had* to die. "Without shedding of blood, there is no forgiveness" (Heb. 9:22). God's sacrificial system demanded a blood atonement, for "the wages of sin is death" (Rom. 6:23). Someone must die to pay the price of sin.

That truth leads into what is undoubtedly the most familiar and magnificent statement in all of Scripture: "For God so loved the world,

that He gave His only begotten Son, that whoever believes in Him should not perish, but have
eternal life" (John 3:16). What does it mean to
believe in Christ? It means more than accepting
and affirming the truth of who He is—God in
human flesh—and believing what He says. Real
faith has at its heart a full surrender to Christ.
There is no way to eliminate that truth from
this passage. Jesus does not allow for "faith" that
gives lip service to the truth and then goes ahead
in sin. Look at verses 20–21: "Everyone who does
evil hates the Light, and does not come to the
Light for fear that his deeds will be exposed. But
he who practices the truth comes to the Light, so
that his deeds may be manifested as having been
wrought in God."

Verse 36 goes even further, equating disobedience with unbelief: "He who believes in
the Son has eternal life; but he who does not
obey the Son will not see life, but the wrath of
God abides on him." Thus the test of true faith
is this: *Does it produce obedience?* If not, it is not
saving faith. Disobedience is unbelief. Real faith
obeys.

John 3:17 is another rebuke to the religious
system Nicodemus represented. The Pharisees
were looking for a Messiah who would come to

destroy the Gentiles and set up a utopia for the Jews. But Jesus said, "God did not send the Son into the world to judge the world, but that the world might be saved through Him." Those who thought the coming of the Messiah meant glory for Israel and destruction for everybody else were going to be disappointed. He came to bring salvation not just to Israel, but to the whole world. That is the reality of redemption. It is offered not just to Pharisees, not just to the Jews, but to "whoever believes in Him" (v. 16).

Jesus made this wonderful promise to sinners: "He who believes in Him is not judged" (John 3:18). He balanced it with a chilling warning to the Pharisees and all others who reject Christ: "He who does not believe has been judged already, because he has not believed in the name of the only begotten Son of God." Condemnation for unbelievers is not relegated to the future. What will be consummated in the final judgment has already begun. "This is the judgment, that the Light has come into the world, and men loved the darkness rather than the Light; for their deeds were evil" (v. 19). Having hated and rejected the light, those whose deeds are evil consign themselves to eternal darkness.

Don't miss the exclusivity of the gospel. There is only one way to gain a right standing with God. You cannot earn it for yourself. Jesus—*only Jesus*—is the sole source of salvation. Those who do not believe in His name are condemned, excluded from eternal life. No matter how sincere, how religious, how immersed in good works, everyone must be born again. There is no promise of life—only a guarantee of condemnation—for those who will not identify with the sinful, dying Israelites and turn from sin in obedient faith to the One who was lifted up so that they would not have to perish.

CHAPTER 4

In Spirit and in Truth

The message of Christ rebukes both the self-righteousness of a Pharisee and the lascivious lifestyle of a wanton adulterer. Christ's ministry in John 3 and 4 covered both ends of the moral spectrum.

John 4 contains one of the most familiar and beautiful conversations in all Scripture. Here our Lord offers salvation to an outcast woman as if He were handing her a drink of water. But do not mistake His straightforward offer for a shallow message.

Jesus, knowing the woman's heart, understood exactly what message she needed to hear to be brought to faith. He made no mention of sin's wages, repentance, faith, atonement, His death for sin, or His resurrection. Are we to conclude that those are not essential elements of the gospel message? Certainly not.

The woman was uniquely prepared by the Holy Spirit for this moment. Unlike Nicodemus, she was no theologian, but her heart was ready to acknowledge her sin and embrace Christ. His message to her was meant to draw her to Himself, not to provide a comprehensive gospel outline intended to be normative for every episode of personal evangelism. We must learn from our Lord's methods, but we cannot isolate this passage and try to draft a model for a universal gospel presentation from it.

All we know about the woman's background is that her life was a tangle of adulteries and broken marriages. In her society, that would have made her a spurned outcast, with no more social status than a common prostitute. She seemed anything but a prime target for conversion. To call her to Himself, Jesus had to force her to face her indifference, lust, self-centeredness, immorality, and religious prejudice.

The woman makes a vivid contrast to Nicodemus. They were virtual opposites.

Nicodemus was a Jew; she was a Samaritan. He was a man; she was a woman. He was a religious leader; she was an adulteress. He was learned; she was ignorant. He was a member of the highest class; she of the lowest—lower even than an outcast of Israel, for she was a Samaritan outcast. He was wealthy; she was poor. He recognized Jesus as a teacher from God; she didn't have a clue who He was. The two of them could hardly have been more dissimilar.

But it was the same powerful and omniscient Christ who revealed Himself to her. Take note; this is not primarily the tale of a Samaritan woman. Rather, this is the account of Jesus' self-revelation as Messiah. Of all occasions for Jesus to disclose who He was, He chose to tell this unknown woman of Samaria first. We might wonder why He didn't go to downtown Jerusalem, walk into the temple, and there announce to the assembled leaders that He was the Messiah. Why would He reveal it first to an obscure, adulterous woman?

Certainly He intended to demonstrate that the gospel was for the whole world, not just the Hebrew race, and that His ministry was to poor outcasts as well as the religious elite. It was a rebuke to the Jewish leaders that their

Messiah ignored them and disclosed Himself to a Samaritan adulteress. When He finally did unveil the truth to Israel's leaders, they didn't believe it anyway.

We are told only the barest essentials of the Lord's conversation with the woman. Scripture reveals nothing specific about her thoughts or emotions. We are given no insight into how much she understood—or if she understood at all—about the Lord's offer to give her living water. It is not clear when she realized He was actually speaking about spiritual life. The only insight we have into the response of her heart is what we infer from her words and actions.

In fact, although we assume she embraced Christ as Messiah and became a believer, even that is not explicitly stated in the text. We make that judgment on the basis of her behavior—specifically the fact that she ran to tell others about Him, and they believed.

So we must be careful to realize that this passage alone is not an appropriate foundation upon which to build a complete understanding of all vital gospel truth. Unlike us, Jesus knew the woman's heart. As He spoke to her, He could judge her response and know exactly how much she understood and believed. He was able to bear down on precisely the truth she needed to hear; He used no canned presentation or four-point outline of gospel facts.

Nevertheless, Jesus' discourse with the Samaritan woman establishes some clear guidelines for personal evangelism. As the master evangelist seeks to win her, He expertly directs the conversation, taking her from a simple comment about drinking water to a revelation that He is the Messiah. Along the way, He skillfully avoids her attempts to control the conversation, change the subject, and ask irrelevant questions. Five lessons in particular stand out as critical truths to be emphasized in presenting the way of salvation.

The Lesson of the Well: Christ Came to Seek and Save the Lost

Notice the events that led to this encounter. Jesus had left Judea and was on His way to Galilee (John 4:3). Verse 1 tells us that the word was out about His success. Masses of people were flocking to see Him. That created a severe problem. The Jewish leaders hated John the Baptist because he taught the truth and thus condemned them, so you can imagine what they thought of Jesus Christ. The more people came to see Jesus, the more uncomfortable the religious leaders grew. In fact, from this point on in the ministry of Christ, His running battle with the Pharisees is a constant theme. It finally culminated in their putting Him to death.

Jesus left Judea, not because He was afraid of the Pharisees, but because it was not God's time for a confrontation. He also had a positive reason for leaving: "He had to pass through Samaria" (John 4:4). This was not a geographical necessity. In fact, traveling through Samaria was not normal for a Jew. The Samaritans were so offensive to them that they wanted nothing less than to set foot in Samaria. Although the most direct route went straight through Samaria, the Jews never went that way. They had their own trail, which went to the north of Judea, east of the Jordan, then back into Galilee. Jesus could have followed that well-traveled route from Judea to Galilee.

But by journeying instead through Samaria, our Lord was displaying His love for sinners. The Samaritans were hybrid Jews who had married into the surrounding nations when Israel was taken into captivity in 722 BC (cf. 2 Kings

17:23–25). They rejected Jerusalem as the center of worship and built their own temple on Mount Gerizim in Samaria. Their intermarriage and idolatry were deemed evils so gross that orthodox Jewish people ordinarily had no dealings with them (John 4:9). Samaria had essentially become a separate nation, viewed by the Jews as more abhorrent than the Gentiles. This hatred and bitterness between Jews and Samaritans had gone on for centuries. Merely by traveling through Samaria, our Lord was shattering age-old barriers.

The reason He *had* to go that way was to fulfill a divine appointment at Jacob's well. He had come to seek and to save the lost (Luke 19:10), and even if it meant a serious breach of cultural protocol, He would be there when the time was right. And His timing was critical. Had He arrived at that well ten minutes early or late, he might have missed this woman. But His schedule was perfect; He wrote the script Himself even before the foundation of the world.

Christ arrived at the appointed place, a plot of ground Jacob had purchased and given to Joseph. John 4:6 says, "Jesus, being wearied from His journey, was sitting thus by the well. It was about the sixth hour." Here we get a glimpse of the humanity of Christ. Because He was a man in every sense, He was weary. The writer of Hebrews says He was touched with the feelings of our infirmities (Heb. 4:15).

John probably used the Roman system of marking time. Roman time began at noon, so the sixth hour would be six o'clock. The people in Sychar would be finished with their work, and the women would be doing the daily chore of drawing water. Our Lord had reached the end of a long, hot journey under the sun, and He was tired and thirsty. He was at the appointed place, in God's timing, determined to do God's will. He was there to seek and to save a single pathetic, wretched woman.

The Lesson of the Woman: God Is No Respecter of Persons

"There came a woman of Samaria to draw water" (John 4:7). This woman was a moral outcast, ostracized from society. Imagine her shock when Jesus said to her, "Give Me a drink" (v. 7). Not only was she used to being shunned by everyone, but in that culture, men did not speak publicly with women—even their wives. Furthermore,

Jesus had shattered the racial barrier. She was startled that Jesus had spoken to her and even more shocked that He would ask for a drink from her "unclean" vessel. She asked, "How is it that You, being a Jew, ask me for a drink since I am a Samaritan woman?" (v. 9).

God is no respecter of persons (Acts 10:34), and Jesus was not ashamed to take a drink from the vessel of a woman for whom He had come to die. Nobody—not this woman, not a Pharisee like Nicodemus, not even the most loathsome leper—was beyond the reach of His divine love.

The Lesson of the Water: Everyone Who Thirsts May Come

"Jesus answered and said to her, 'If you knew the gift of God, and who it is who says to you, "Give Me a drink," you would have asked Him, and He would have given you living water'" (John 4:10). Suddenly He turned the situation around. At first He was thirsty and she had the water. Now He was speaking to her as if she were the thirsty one and He had the water. Instead of asking for a drink, He declared that she needed a drink from His fountain. The issue was no longer His physical thirst, but her spiritual need. Though she apparently did not understand yet, He was offering living water for her dry soul.

The living water He held out to her was the gift of salvation including all that is inherent in the reality of redemption—freedom from sin, the commitment to follow Jesus, the ability to obey God's law, and the power and desire to live a life that glorifies Him.

But she still seemed to be thinking in terms of literal water. "She said to Him, 'Sir, You have nothing to draw with and the well is deep; where then do You get that living water? You are not greater than our father Jacob, are You, who gave us the well, and drank of it himself and his sons and his cattle?'" (John 4:11–12).

If only she knew—He was *incomparably* greater than Jacob and His water *infinitely* better than Jacob's water. He tried to explain more about the unique properties of His living water: "Everyone who drinks of this water will thirst again; but whoever drinks of the water that I will give him shall never thirst; but the water that I will give him will become in him a well of water springing up to eternal life" (vv. 13–14). This was water to quench a parched soul.

Her response was immediate: "Sir, give me

this water, so I will not be thirsty nor come all the way here to draw" (v. 15). Apparently she still was somewhat confused about whether He meant literal water or something spiritual. Either way, she wanted this living water!

Notice, however, that at this juncture, even though she *did* ask for it, Jesus did not simply give her the Water of Life. She asked for it and presumably would have accepted it had He given it outright. But Jesus was not looking for a cheap pseudo-conversion. He knew she was not yet ready for living water. There were two issues that needed to be addressed first: her sin and His true identity.

Jesus never sanctioned any form of cheap grace. He was not offering eternal life as an add-on to a life cluttered with unconfessed sin. It is inconceivable that He would pour someone a drink of living water without challenging and altering that individual's sinful lifestyle. He came to save His people *from their sin* (cf. Matt. 1:21), not to confer immortality on people in bondage to wickedness (cf. Gen. 3:22–24).

The Lord went right to the heart of the issue—by letting her know she could not cloak her sin: "Go, call your husband and come here" (John 4:16). It was a loaded remark. The web of this woman's adulteries was so complex and her sin so great that she did not even try to explain. "I have no husband" (v. 17) was all she replied.

Jesus knew the full truth anyway: "You have correctly said, 'I have no husband'; for you have had five husbands, and the one whom you now have is not your husband; this you have said truly" (vv. 17–18). Imagine her shame when she realized He knew all about her sin! Certainly she would have preferred to keep it hidden. She had not lied to Him, but she hadn't told the whole truth, either. It is as if Jesus said, "All right, if you're not going to confess your own sin, I'm going to confront you by telling you what it is."

Then she *did* confess her sin. By saying, "Sir, I perceive that You are a prophet" (v. 19), she was, in effect, saying, "You are right. That's me. That's my sinful life. What you said about me is true."

Jesus had peeled back the camouflage from all her sin. And yet, even with full knowledge of her depravity, He was offering *her* the Water of Life! If she had known the Scriptures well, Isaiah 55:1 might have come to mind: "Ho! Every one who thirsts, come to the waters." The offer of living water is not just to religious people like Nicodemus—*everyone* who thirsts is invited to drink deeply of the living water—even an adulterous woman whose life is fraught with sin.

Isaiah adds a charge to sinners, along with a wonderful promise that would have gladdened the Samaritan woman's heart:

> Let the wicked forsake his way,
> And the unrighteous man his
>   thoughts;
> And let him return to the LORD,
> And He will have compassion on him,
> And to our God,
> For He will abundantly pardon.
>   ISAIAH 55:7

The Lesson of True Worship:
Now Is the Acceptable Time

Having recognized Him as more than a mere traveling man, the woman asked the first spiritual question that came to mind: "Our fathers worshiped in this mountain, and you people say that in Jerusalem is the place where men ought to worship" (John 4:20). Since He was a genuine prophet, He ought to know which group was right!

Jesus' response, like His answer to Nicodemus, cut through the woman's misplaced interest and confronted her with her *real* need—forgiveness. "Woman, believe Me," He told her, "an hour is coming when neither in this mountain nor in Jerusalem will you worship the Father" (v. 21). Then, almost incidentally, He told her that the Jews were right and the Samaritans were wrong: "You worship that which you do not know; we worship that which we know; for salvation is from the Jews" (v. 22). If only she had known it, the Jew she was speaking to was the One who came to bring salvation!

The *where* of worship is not really the issue; it is *who*, *when*, and *how* that really count. Jesus said, "An hour is coming, and now is, when the true worshipers will worship the Father in spirit and truth; for such people the Father seeks to be His worshipers. God is spirit, and those who worship Him must worship in spirit and truth" (vv. 23–24). True worship occurs not on a mountain or in a temple, but in the inner person.

The phrase "an hour is coming and now is" gave Jesus' words a sense of immediacy and personal meaning to this woman. It was as if He were saying, "You don't have to go up to the mountain or down to Jerusalem to worship. You can worship here and now." Having brought her to the threshold of eternal life, He was affirming the urgency of salvation: "Behold, now is 'the acceptable time,' behold, now is 'the day of salvation'" (2 Cor. 6:2). The Messiah was present; the day of salvation had arrived; and this was not only the Messiah's time, but her time too.

It is significant that Jesus used the expression "true worshipers" to refer to the body of redeemed people. All who are saved are true worshipers. There is no possibility of being saved and yet *not* worshiping God in Spirit and truth. God's objective in salvation is to create a true worshiper (cf. Phil. 3:3). Our Lord had come into the world to seek and to save the lost. He revealed to a Samaritan woman that His objective in seeking and redeeming sinners is to fulfill God's will in making them true worshipers. Then He invited her to become one.

When Jesus said the Father was seeking true worshipers, it was more than a statement of fact. It was a personal invitation to the Samaritan woman. Do not miss the importance of that invitation. It debunks the notion that Jesus was offering eternal life without making any demand for a spiritual commitment. The Lord of glory does not say "come to the waters" apart from the command, "let the wicked forsake his way" (cf. Isa. 55:1, 7). The call to worship the Father in spirit and in truth was a clear summons to the deepest and most comprehensive kind of spiritual submission.

But the woman was still confused, and one can hardly blame her. She had come to the well to get a simple pot of water, and in a brief conversation, her sin had been exposed and she was challenged to become a true worshiper of the living God. Her heart longed for someone who could take her tangled thoughts and emotions and make some sense out of everything. So she told Jesus, "I know that Messiah is coming . . .; when that One comes, He will declare all things to us" (John 4:25).

Jesus' reply must have shaken her to the core: "I who speak to you am He" (v. 26). What a dynamic confrontation! This Man who had asked her for a simple cup of water was now standing there, claiming to be the true Messiah, holding forth living water and promising to forgive her sin and transform her into a true worshiper of the living God!

Although the text does not specifically tell us she became a believer, it seems obvious she did. I believe she embraced Him as Messiah and Savior, somewhere in the white space between verses 26 and 27. The hour of salvation had come for her. She would willingly become a true worshiper. She would drink of the Water of Life. The irresistible grace of the Messiah had penetrated her heart. Step by step He had opened her sinful heart and disclosed Himself to her; and apparently she responded with saving faith.

The Lesson of the Witness:
This Man Receives Sinners

The disciples had been in the village buying food, and John tells us they returned "at this point" (John 4:27). The Greek expression means "precisely at this moment." Apparently they came back just when the Lord said, "I who speak to you am He." Had they arrived any later, they would not have heard the declaration of His messiahship. It must have shocked them to hear Him telling this outcast Samaritan woman that He was the Messiah, since He had never previously told anyone that. John says, "They were amazed that He had been speaking with a woman, yet no one said, 'What do You seek?' or, 'Why do You speak with her?'" (v. 27).

The woman's actions at this point strongly indicate that she had become a believer. She "left her waterpot, and went into the city and said to the men, 'Come, see a man who told me all the things that I have done; this is not the Christ, is it?'" (vv. 28–29). She evidenced all the characteristics of genuine conversion. She had sensed her need, she had confessed her guilt, she recognized Jesus as Messiah, and now she was showing the fruit of her transformed life by bringing other people to Him.

It is significant that her first impulse as a new believer was to go and tell others about Christ. The desire to proclaim one's faith is a common experience of new believers. In fact, some of the most zealous witnesses for Christ are brand-new believers. That is because their minds are fresh with the memory of the weight of their guilt and the exhilaration of being loosed from it. That was the case with this woman. The first thing she declared to the men of the town was that Jesus had told her everything she ever did. He had held her sin up to the light and compelled her to face who she really was. Then He had released her from the shame. That she talked so freely about it shows she had been liberated from the bondage of her guilt.

Jesus had given her a drink of the Water of Life, and she had begun to worship God in spirit and truth. She didn't need to conceal her guilt anymore; she was forgiven.

The way the woman phrased her question seems to imply a negative answer: "This is not the Christ, is it?" But it was not an expression of doubt. If she had come into town and said, "Men, I've found the Messiah," the men would have either ignored her or laughed her out of town. She, an outcast adulteress, was not the most qualified person in town to identify the Messiah. Besides, women didn't tell men anything in that society. So she put it in the form of a question—really a discreet challenge to them. That way they would meet Him with an open mind. She knew Christ would do the rest.

The woman's testimony had a profound impact on the village. Scripture tells us, "From that city many of the Samaritans believed in Him because of the word of the woman who testified, 'He told me all the things that I have done'" (John 4:39). It was the news of how He had uncovered her sin that made such a deep impression. Others, too, responded to Him with zeal (vv. 40–42).

The reason for such a passionate reaction was that the people were Samaritans. In a sense, they all were in the same boat as the woman. They knew the Messiah was coming to set things right, and most of them probably anticipated His coming with fear. Their perspective was the exact opposite of the Pharisees'. The Jewish leaders were looking for a conquering victor who would take up their cause and destroy their enemies. The Samaritans had no such expectation. If the Jews were right, they would be the targets of Messiah's wrath.

So when this woman came and announced to the people of Sychar that One claiming to be the Messiah had dealt mercifully with her although He knew all her sin, their hearts embraced Him enthusiastically.

Contrast their reaction with that of the Pharisees, described in Luke 15:2: "Both the Pharisees and the scribes began to grumble, saying, 'This man receives sinners.'" In essence, that is precisely what the Samaritan woman told the men of Sychar: "He is the Messiah, but He receives sinners!" What was repugnant to the scribes and Pharisees was good news to these

Samaritans, because they were willing to admit they were sinners.

It was Jesus Himself who said, "I did not come to call the righteous, but sinners" (Matt. 9:13). Those who refused to acknowledge their sin found Him to be a Judge, not a Savior. He never gave such people any encouragement, any comfort, or any reason to hope. The Water of Life He held forth was given only to those who acknowledged the hopelessness of their sinful state.

God seeks people who will submit themselves to worship Him in spirit and in truth. That kind of worship is impossible for those sheltering sin in their lives. Those who confess and forsake their sin, on the other hand, will find a Savior eager to receive them, forgive them, and liberate them from their sin. Like the woman at the well, they will find a source of living water that will quench forever even the strongest spiritual thirst.

The final chapter of the Bible closes with this invitation, which evokes a picture of the Samaritan woman: "Let the one who is thirsty come; let the one who wishes take the water of life without cost" (Rev. 22:17). While it is free, it is not cheap; the Savior Himself paid the ultimate price so that thirsty, repentant seekers can drink as deeply as they like.

CHAPTER 5

Good News
for Sinners

Too many Christians in this media-driven era think of evangelism as a marketing challenge where they must "sell" the gospel by making it sound as easy and attractive as possible. They labor to sound as politically correct, seeker sensitive, ego-affirming, and agreeable as possible. But the product of that goal is a message that fails to confront individuals with the reality of their sin. This leads to spurious "faith" and unconverted church members. As a result, even the most conservative churches are teeming with people who, claiming to be born again, live like pagans.

But contemporary Christians have been

conditioned never to question anyone's profession of faith. Multitudes declare that they trust Christ as Savior while indulging in lifestyles that are plainly inconsistent with God's Word—yet no one dares to challenge their testimony.

I once spent time with a fellow minister who drove me through his city. We passed a large liquor store, and I happened to mention that it was an unusual-looking place.

"Yes," he said. "There is a whole chain of those stores around the city, all owned by one man. He is a member of my Sunday school class."

I wondered aloud how such a thing could be, and the minister replied, "Oh, he's quite faithful. He is in class every week."

"Does it bother him that he owns all those liquor stores?" I asked.

"We've talked about it some," he said. "But he feels people are going to buy liquor anyway, so why not buy it from him?"

I asked, "What is his life like?"

"Well, he did leave his wife and is living with a young girl," the minister replied. Then after several minutes of my bewildered and uncomfortable silence, he added, "You know, sometimes it's hard for me to understand how a Christian can live like that."

I must confess that it is hard for me to understand how someone who teaches the Bible can assume that a man living in wanton rebellion against God's standards is a Christian merely because he claims to be—even if he attends Sunday school every week.

Coming to Grips with Sin

Many Christians today have the idea that salvation is only the granting of eternal life, not necessarily the liberation of a sinner from the bondage of his iniquity. We tell people that God loves them and has a wonderful plan for their lives, but that is only half the truth. God also hates sin and will punish unrepentant sinners with eternal torment. No gospel presentation is complete if it avoids or conceals those facts. Any message that fails to define and confront the severity of personal sin is a deficient gospel. And any "salvation" that does not alter a lifestyle of sin and transform the heart of the sinner is not the salvation God's Word speaks of.

Sin is no peripheral issue as far as salvation is concerned; it is *the* issue. In fact, the distinctive element of the Christian message is the power of Jesus Christ to forgive and conquer our sin. Of all the realities of the gospel, none is more wonderful than the news that the enslaving grasp of sin has been broken. This truth is the heart and the very lifeblood of the Christian message.

It is absurd to suggest that a person can encounter the holy God of Scripture and be saved without also coming to grips with the heinousness of sin and consequently longing to turn from it. In the Bible, those who met God were invariably confronted with an overwhelming sense of their own sinfulness. Peter, seeing Jesus for who He was, said, "Go away from me Lord, for I am a sinful man!" (Luke 5:8). Paul wrote, "It is a trustworthy statement, deserving full acceptance, that Christ Jesus came into the world *to save sinners*, among whom I am foremost of all" (1 Tim. 1:15). Job, whom God Himself identified as a righteous man (Job 1:1, 8), said after seeing God face-to-face, "I abhor myself, and repent in dust and ashes" (Job 42:6 KJV). Isaiah, seeing God, gasped, "Woe is me, for I am ruined! Because I am a man of unclean lips, and I live among a people of unclean lips; for my eyes have seen the King, the LORD of hosts" (Isa. 6:5). There are many other examples of men and women in Scripture who, having seen God, feared for their own lives—always because they were smitten with the weight of their own sin. It is appropriate, then, that when Matthew relates his own conversion experience, the central truth that emerges is Christ's mercy to sinners.

Matthew 9:9–13 describes the incident, along with the controversy that ensued. In one of the most important statements ever recorded in the Bible, the Lord says, "I did not come to call the righteous, but sinners" (v. 13). This statement contains a full perspective on Jesus' ministry, a summary of the message of Christianity, a close-up of the nucleus of the gospel, and the basic rationale behind the incarnation.

Why did Jesus come into the world? To call sinners—those who know they have a terminal disease, those who are hopeless and desperate, those who are hurting, those who are hungry and thirsty, those who are weak and weary, those who are broken, those whose lives are shattered, those who are desperate—sinners who know they are unworthy yet long to be forgiven.

Jesus' words were aimed at the self-righteous Pharisees, who, like many today, thought they were righteous and without any real spiritual need. The truth is that unless people realize they have a sin problem, they will not come to Christ for a solution. People do not come for healing unless they know they have a disease; they do not come for life unless they are conscious that they are under the penalty of death; they do not come for salvation unless they are weary of the bondage of sin.

Thus Jesus came to expose us all as sinners. That is why His message was so penetrating, so forceful. It tore our self-righteousness away and exposed our evil hearts so that we might see ourselves as sinners.

Receiving Sinners

Throughout his gospel, Matthew argues that Christ is the Messiah of Israel. In chapters 8 and 9 he describes a series of Jesus' miracles categorically selected to show the range of the Messiah's credentials. He lists nine miracles, showing Jesus' power over sickness (8:1–17), over nature (8:23–27), over demons (8:28–34), over death (9:18–26), over blindness (9:27–31), and over a silent tongue (9:32–34).

Matthew's conversion itself falls in among those miracles, right after a spectacular miracle designed to demonstrate Jesus' power over sin

(9:1–8). Christ had just forgiven a paralyzed man's sins, and in a monumental display of His divine authority, He confirmed His deity before the Pharisees by commanding the disabled man to take up his bed and walk. Following immediately on the heels of that narrative, verse 9 describes the call and salvation of Matthew: "As Jesus passed on from there, He saw a man called Matthew, sitting in the tax collector's booth; and He said to him, 'Follow Me!' And he got up and followed Him."

By this account, which is consistent with Mark's and Luke's versions, Jesus spoke only two words to him: "Follow Me!" And Matthew obeyed. Luke 5:28 adds this significant statement: "And he left everything behind." He forsook all to follow Christ. Matthew was too humble to say that about himself, but Luke did—and it speaks volumes about the nature of Matthew's conversion. He paid a great price, perhaps a higher price than any of the other disciples. A fisherman who followed Jesus could always go back to fishing. But a tax collector who left his station was finished, because the next day Rome would have someone else to take his place. Yet Matthew forsook everything immediately. He didn't say, "Well, I'm coming

Lord—but, hey, I could finance this whole operation if You'd just let me grab these bags!" He turned his back on it all, forsaking everything he had.

Matthew was a major sinner, and everyone knew it. By the standards of his day, he was unequivocally the vilest, most wretched sinner in Capernaum. He was a publican, a willing tool of the Roman government, employed in the odious task of squeezing tax money out of his own people. Publicans would buy franchises from Rome. That gave them the right to collect taxes in a certain town or district. By buying into the Roman system, Matthew had revealed himself as a traitor to Israel. Nothing in the mind of the Jewish people was more offensive. He had hired on to the conquering pagans who oppressed his own people and in doing so established his reputation as the worst kind of turncoat, heretic, and renegade.

Rome required each publican to collect a certain amount of taxes. Anything they acquired after that, they could keep. The Roman government, in order to keep their tax collectors happy and productive, supported them in the wildest excesses and abuses. They virtually had a free hand to overcharge people and extort whatever they could from their countrymen. A shrewd publican could amass a huge fortune in very little time—all at the expense of his own oppressed brethren. Understandably, they were regarded with the utmost contempt by all Israel.

Publicans were so despised by the Jews that they were barred from the synagogues. They were regarded as unclean beasts, treated like swine. They could not be witnesses in any court of law because they were not to be trusted. They were known as flagrant liars, classified with robbers and murderers.

Most Jews believed it was wrong to pay taxes to Rome. Looking backward to an Old Testament theocracy, they believed only God should receive their money. That is why the Pharisees tested Jesus, attempting to bring Him into disfavor either with Rome or with the people by asking Him whether it was right to pay taxes (Matt. 22:15–22).

Matthew had authority to collect taxes on almost everything. In addition to import and export taxes, he was free to assess bridge tolls, harbor fees, and road-use taxes. He could open every package coming along the road. He could even open private letters to see if business was being conducted. If so, he could also tax that.

His office was located at the confluence of two roads, probably right at the north port of the Sea of Galilee. That would have put him at a strategic point on the road from Damascus, where he could tax everyone going east and west. He also could tax the area's highly productive fishing industry.

Note that Matthew was sitting at the tax table. Some publicans, concerned about their reputations, stayed out of the public eye by hiring others to collect taxes for them. But the really brash ones—the ones who did not care what people thought of them—actually sat at the table themselves rather than paying someone else to do it. It was one thing to be a publican; it was worse to flaunt it. Rabbinical tradition said it was impossible for a man in his position to repent. You can imagine the gasps from the crowd when Jesus stopped before Matthew and said, "Follow Me."

Matthew must have been a man under conviction. Deep down in his heart he must have longed to be free from his life of sin, and that must have been why he virtually ran to join Christ. Because it meant giving up so much, he would never have followed Jesus on a whim. He surely knew what he was getting into. Jesus had ministered publicly all over that area; everyone in the vicinity of Capernaum knew who He was and what He taught. They had seen His miracles, signs, and wonders. Matthew was familiar with Jesus' rigorous demands for discipleship (Matt. 8:18–22). He knew what he was being recruited for. He had counted the cost and was prepared to follow.

Eating with Tax-Gatherers and Sinners

Matthew decided to have a banquet to introduce Jesus to his friends. Like most new believers, he wanted to bring everyone he knew to Christ. Luke 5:29 reveals that Matthew (who was also known as Levi) held the banquet in his own house. Jesus was the honored guest. This gathering was attended by some of the most villainous people in the history of banquets. The only people Matthew knew were sordid types, wretched sinners, because no one else would associate with him. The respectable people despised him. His friends were thieves, blasphemers, prostitutes, con artists, swindlers, and other tax collectors—the riffraff of society.

Supercilious religious types would say, of course, that Jesus shouldn't go to a banquet with such degenerates. That is exactly what the Pharisees thought. But that was not the way of the Savior. Matthew 11:19 indicates that He was known among the people as "a friend of tax collectors and sinners." This very banquet probably gave rise to that perception. The Pharisees meant it derisively, but it was nonetheless a fitting title for the Son of Man.

Matthew 9:10 sets the scene: "It happened that as Jesus was reclining at the table in the house, behold, many tax collectors and sinners came and were dining with Jesus and His disciples." This was so scandalous to the self-righteous Pharisees that they could hardly conceal their shock. *If he were really the Messiah, they thought, he would be having a dinner for us!*

Apparently the Pharisees lingered outside until the banquet was over. Avoiding a head-on confrontation with Jesus, they cornered the disciples and asked, "Why is your Teacher eating with the tax collectors and sinners?" (v. 11). Rather than an honest question, this was a veiled rebuke, a venting of their bitterness.

On overhearing their conversation, Jesus

had His own rebuke: "It is not those who are healthy who need a physician, but those who are sick. But go and learn what this means: 'I desire compassion, and not sacrifice,' for I did not come to call the righteous, but sinners" (vv. 12–13). Jesus' answer is a powerful threefold argument, first appealing to human experience, then arguing from Scripture, and finally resting on His own divine authority.

Jesus' appeal to experience compares sinners to sick people who need a doctor. The analogy is simple: a physician can be expected to visit the ill (or at least that was the case in Jesus' day), so a forgiver should be expected to visit people who sin. It came as a stinging rebuke to the hard-heartedness of the Pharisees: "If you're so perceptive as to diagnose them as sinners, what are you going to do about it? Or are you doctors who give diagnoses but no cure?" Thus He exposed the Pharisees as pious critics who freely defined others as sinners but were utterly indifferent to their plight.

Jesus' argument from Scripture blasted the Pharisees' pride: "Go and learn" (v. 13). This phrase was used in the rabbinic writings to reprove students who were ignorant about something they should have known. It was like saying, "Go back through the books and come again when you've got the basic information." He quotes Hosea 6:6, "I delight in loyalty rather than sacrifice." In other words, God is not concerned with ritual (ceremony) but with compassion, mercy, and loving-kindness (character). The Pharisees, good at ritual, had no love for sinners. God had instituted the sacrificial system and had ordered Israel to follow prescribed rituals, but that was pleasing to God only when it was the expression of a broken and contrite heart (Ps. 51:16–17). When the heart was not right, the ritual was an abomination. God is never pleased with forms of religion apart from personal righteousness.

The third argument, from His own authority, leveled the Pharisees: "I did not come to call the righteous, but sinners" (v. 13). Luke 5:32 adds the words, "to repentance." Luke 18:9 describes the Pharisees as "some people who trusted in themselves that they were righteous, and viewed others with contempt." Here, in essence, Jesus is saying to them, "You say you're righteous, and I accept that as your self-evaluation. But if that's the case, I have nothing to say to you, for I have come to call sinners to repentance."

The Greek word translated "call" here is *kaleō*, a word often used for inviting a guest into one's home. Such an invitation is found in Matthew 22:1–14, a parable that fits perfectly with Jesus' words to these Pharisees. There, Jesus pictured His kingdom as a banquet. A king sent invitations calling all his friends to a wedding banquet for his son, but everyone who was invited refused to come. So the king told his servants to invite anyone they could find. These pious, cold-hearted, self-righteous Pharisees were like those who refused to come to the banquet. They would not acknowledge their sin, so they could not respond to Jesus' call. After all, Jesus came to call sinners to repentance.

Refusing the Righteous

God receives sinners. The flip side of that truth is that He refuses the righteous. Not that there are any truly righteous people, of course (Rom. 3:10). But those who think they are good enough—those who do not understand the seriousness of sin—cannot respond to the gospel. They cannot be saved, for the gospel is a call to sinners to repent and be forgiven. These are frightening words: "I did not come to call the righteous." The unmistakable message is that Christ's gracious call to salvation is not extended to those who view themselves as righteous.

From the beginning of Jesus' ministry, the heart of His message was a call to repentance. In fact, when our Lord first began to preach, the opening word of His message was "Repent" (Matt. 4:17). It was also the first word of John the Baptist's message (Matt. 3:2) and the basis of the gospel the apostles preached (Acts 3:19; 20:21; 26:20). No one who neglects to call sinners to repentance is preaching the gospel accurately.

Now and then a preacher will smugly say that he does not preach on sin because it is too negative. A few years ago, a well-known preacher sent me a book he had written in which he redefined sin as nothing more than a poor self-image. The way to reach people, he said, is to bolster their self-esteem, not to make them think of themselves as sinful. There is no gospel in a message like that! Rather than bringing people to salvation, it confirms them in the self-condemning vanity of their own egos.

Christ's call to salvation and discipleship is extended only to desperate sinners who realize their need and desire transformation. Our Lord came to save sinners. But to those who are unwilling to admit their sin, He has nothing to say—except to pronounce judgment.

CHAPTER 6

To Seek and
Save the Lost

There is no more glorious truth in the Bible than the words of Luke 19:10: "The Son of Man has come to seek and to save that which was lost." That verse sums up the work of Christ on earth. From the human viewpoint, it may represent the single most important truth ever recorded in Scripture.

Jesus' sermons were not manifestos for social reform or political revolution. The essence of His message was always the gospel of salvation. He said of His own mission, "I have not come to call the righteous but sinners to repentance" (Luke 5:32). The apostle Paul said in 1 Timothy 1:15, "It

is a trustworthy statement, deserving full acceptance, that Christ Jesus came into the world to save
sinners, among whom I am foremost of all."

Search and Rescue

The nature of God is to seek and to save sinners. From the opening pages of human history,
it was God who sought the fallen couple in the
Garden. In Ezekiel 34:16 God says, "I will seek
the lost, bring back the scattered, bind up the
broken and strengthen the sick." The Almighty
was portrayed as a Savior throughout the Old
Testament (Ps. 106:21; Isa. 43:11; Hos. 13:4), so
it is appropriate that when Christ entered the
world of human beings as God in human flesh,
He was known first of all as a Savior.

Even Jesus' name was divinely chosen to
be the name of a Savior. An angel told Joseph
in a dream, "You shall call His name Jesus, for
He will save His people from their sins" (Matt.
1:21). The very heart of all redemptive teaching
is that Jesus entered this world on a search and
rescue mission for sinners. That truth is what
characterizes the gospel as good news.

But it is good news only for those who perceive themselves as sinners. The unequivocal teaching of Jesus is that those who will not acknowledge and repent of their sin are beyond the reach of saving grace. All are sinners, but not all are willing to admit their depravity. If they do, Jesus becomes their friend (cf. Matt. 11:19). If they will not, they will know Him only as Judge (cf. Matt. 7:22).

Again, Jesus' parable in Luke 18:10–13 underscores this truth. He directed these words at "some people who trusted in themselves that they were righteous, and viewed others with contempt" (v. 9):

Two men went up into the temple to pray, one a Pharisee and the other a tax collector. The Pharisee stood and was praying this to himself, "God, I thank You that I am not like other people: swindlers, unjust, adulterers, or even like this tax collector. I fast twice a week; I pay tithes of all that I get." But the tax collector, standing some distance away, was even unwilling to lift up his eyes to heaven, but was beating

his breast, saying, "God, be merciful to
me, the sinner!"

Our Lord's assessment of those two men
must have bewildered and infuriated His audience of self-righteous Pharisees: "I tell you, this
man [the tax collector] went to his house justified rather than the other; for everyone who
exalts himself will be humbled, but he who
humbles himself will be exalted" (v. 14).

Humble repentance is the only acceptable
response to the gospel. Those who fail to confess their sin He turns away. But He reaches out
in grace to those who, like Matthew and the
Samaritan woman, admit their sinfulness and
seek deliverance. The worse the sinner, the more
marvelously His grace and glory are revealed
through that sinner's redemption.

Multitudes of repentant sinners responded
during Jesus' earthly ministry. He continually
ministered to tax collectors and other outcasts.
Luke 15:1 indicates that a constant stream of such
people approached Him. In fact, the Pharisees'
worst complaint about His ministry was, "This
man receives sinners and eats with them" (Luke
15:2). They set themselves in contrast and were
condemned by their own comparison. They had

no heart for the outcast, no love for the sinner, no compassion for the lost. Worse, they had no sense of their own sinfulness. Christ could do nothing for them.

The Setting for a Miracle

Like Matthew, Zaccheus was a tax-gatherer whose heart was divinely prepared to receive and follow Christ. His encounter with Jesus took place in Jericho, as the Lord was passing through on His way to Jerusalem to die. Jesus had for some time been ministering in Galilee. His hometown, Nazareth, was there. He was now headed to Jerusalem for the final Passover, in which He would be the Paschal Lamb, giving His life on the cross for sinners. And as if to show exactly why He had to die, He paused in Jericho to reach out to a wretched tax-gatherer.

Along the journey the Lord had collected an entourage of pilgrims going to celebrate Passover in Jerusalem. His fame had spread throughout Palestine. Not long before this, He had raised Lazarus from the dead. That happened in Bethany, not far from Jericho. Word had spread, and people were curious about Jesus. Everyone in Jericho who could move lined the streets in preparation for His passing through. The city was buzzing. Was He the Messiah? Was He coming to take over? Was He coming to defeat the Romans and set up His kingdom?

Jericho is east and a little north of Jerusalem. It was an international crossroads, located where the main routes north, south, east, and west all came together. The customs house there, where taxes were collected, was a busy place, and Zaccheus was the publican in charge there.

Seeking the Savior

Zaccheus was despised by the whole community. Luke 19:7 says that everyone called him a sinner. Not only was he a tax-gatherer and a traitor to the nation, but this designation "sinner" probably meant that his personal character was debauched as well. That was the case with most publicans.

The Lord Jesus had a special love for tax collectors. Luke especially focuses on the numerous times Jesus encountered them. Luke's theme is the love of the Savior for the lost, and he repeatedly portrays Jesus reaching out to the riffraff of society. Every time Luke mentions a tax collector (3:12; 5:27; 7:29; 15:1; 18:10–13; 19:2), it is in a positive sense. These were the outcasts of a religious society— flagrant public sinners—the very kind Jesus had come to save.

It might appear that Zaccheus was seeking Jesus on his own initiative, but the truth is that if Jesus had not first sought him, he never would have come to the Savior. Sinners never seek God on their own (Rom. 3:11). In our natural, fallen state we are dead in trespasses and sins (Eph. 2:1), excluded from the life of God (4:18), and therefore totally unable and unwilling to seek God. Only when we are touched by the sovereign, convicting power of God do we move toward Him (John 6:44, 65). And thus it is not until God begins to pursue a soul that the soul responds by seeking Him. An anonymous hymn writer penned these words:

> I sought the Lord, and afterward I
> knew
> He moved my soul to seek Him,
> seeking me;
> It was not I that found, O Savior true;
> No, I was found of Thee.

Whenever someone seeks God, you can be certain it is a response to the prompting of a seeking God. We would not love Him if He had not first loved us (cf. 1 John 4:19).

Nevertheless, God invites sinners to seek. Isaiah 55:6 says, "Seek the LORD while He may be found; call upon Him while He is near." Jeremiah 29:13 says, "You will seek Me and find Me when you search for Me with all your heart." God says in Amos 5:4, "Seek Me that you may live." Jesus said, "Seek first His kingdom and His righteousness" (Matt. 6:33) and, "Seek, and you will find" (Matt. 7:7).

Being sought by God, Zaccheus was seeking. He had heard of Jesus but apparently had never seen Him. Luke 19:3 says, "Zaccheus was trying to see who Jesus was." The verb tense implies that he was continually making an effort to see Jesus. Why? Curiosity? Probably. Conscience? Surely. Desire for freedom from guilt? That could be. But beyond all those factors, the reality that he was ultimately saved demonstrates that the central force driving him to Christ was the irresistible convicting power of the Holy Spirit. It is apparent that the Spirit of God had begun in the heart of Zaccheus the process of drawing him to Christ. Zaccheus was not seeking God on his own initiative, but the Spirit of God was moving his heart. In response he made an effort to see Jesus.

Here was an outcast, a hated man, a man whose hands were filled with money he had taken at the expense of poor people. He was a man with tremendous guilt. Yet instead of running and hiding, he desperately wanted to see Jesus. To do this, he overcame a number of obstacles. One was the crowd. The residents of Jericho were already lining the streets. Add to that his small stature. Zaccheus probably judiciously avoided crowds. A short man would have a problem in a crowd to start with. But a short man who was the chief tax commissioner risked getting a well-placed elbow in the jaw, a heavy boot on the big toe, or even a knife in the back.

On this day, Zaccheus was not concerned with such fears. He was not even concerned with his dignity. He was so determined to see Jesus that he ran ahead of the crowd and climbed up into a sycamore tree to await the Savior (Luke 19:4). The sycamore was a short, fat tree with spreading branches. A little person could scurry up the trunk, get out on a limb, and hang over the road. And that is what Zaccheus did. The tree offered a perfect seat for the parade. It was not a dignified place for a man to be, but that was not important to him at this point. Zaccheus only wanted to see Jesus.

The Seeking Savior

What happened next must have staggered Zaccheus. Although Jesus had never met him before, He stopped in the middle of thousands of people, looked up in the tree, and said, "Zaccheus, hurry and come down, for today I must stay at your house" (Luke 19:5). That is known as the direct approach to evangelism! Nothing about Jesus' approach was subtle.

Our Lord had a divinely ordained appointment with the man. "Today I must stay at your house" suggests a mandate, not a request. He was not asking; he was saying, "I'm coming—I *must* come." Zaccheus's heart was prepared according to the divine timetable.

Zaccheus wanted to see Jesus, but he had no idea Jesus wanted to see him. "He hurried and came down and received Him gladly" (v. 6). We might suppose that such a despicable sinner would be distressed to hear the perfect, sinless

Son of God say, "I'm coming to your house," but he was glad. His heart was prepared.

The reaction of the crowd was predictable. Both the religious elite and the common people looked down on Zaccheus. "When they saw it, they all began to grumble, saying, 'He has gone to be the guest of a man who is a sinner'" (v. 7). They believed, as we have seen, that to go into the house of an outcast was to make oneself unclean. To eat with someone like Zaccheus was the worst possible defilement. They placed no value on Zaccheus's soul. They had no concern for his spiritual welfare. Their self-righteous eyes could see only his sin. They could not understand and would not see in their blind pride that Jesus had come to seek and to save sinners, and they condemned Him for it. In doing so, they condemned themselves.

We are never told what happened at Zaccheus's house. Scripture doesn't say what he served for dinner or how long Jesus stayed or what they talked about. Nor do we know what Jesus said to Zaccheus in bringing him to salvation. As we have seen in other accounts where Jesus evangelized, the methodology He used is not the point. Conversion is a divine miracle, and there are no formulas that can bring it about or explain it. There is no four- or five-step plan to salvation or any prefabricated prayer that can guarantee the salvation of a soul.

We can assume that Jesus dealt with the issue of Zaccheus's sin. No doubt Zaccheus already realized what a great sinner he was. Certainly Christ revealed to Zaccheus who He really was—God in the flesh. Whatever He said, He found in Zaccheus an open heart.

The Fruit of Salvation

The curtain seems to rise near the end of their conversation in Luke 19: "Zaccheus stopped and said to the Lord, 'Behold, Lord, half of my possessions I will give to the poor, and if I have defrauded anyone of anything, I will give back four times as much.' And Jesus said to him, 'Today salvation has come to this house, because he, too, is a son of Abraham'" (vv. 8–9).

Notice that Zaccheus addressed Jesus as Lord. That term can mean simply "sir" or "teacher." But here it certainly means more. In verse 9, Jesus said Zaccheus was saved. If so, he must have acknowledged Jesus as Lord God, confessing Him as his own sovereign master.

That is an affirmation he could not have made before Christ worked in his life, and he could not have denied it afterward (cf. 1 Cor. 12:3).

Here is a radically changed man. Deciding to give half his possessions to the poor was a complete reversal. It is clear evidence his heart was transformed. The taker had become a giver. The extortioner had become a philanthropist. He would repay those he had defrauded, giving back four times as much. His mind was changed, his heart was changed, and his clear intention was to change his behavior also. It was not so much that his heart had changed *toward people*, although that surely had happened. But first his heart had changed *toward God*. Now he wanted to obey God by doing what was just and righteous.

It was not necessary for Zaccheus to repay four times as much. Numbers 5:7 required a penalty of one-fifth as restitution for a wrong. But Zaccheus's generosity showed a transformed soul. It is a response typical of a newly redeemed person, the blessed fruit of redemption. He did not say, "Salvation is wonderful, but don't place any demands on my life." There is something in the heart of every newborn believer that wants to obey. It is a heart of eager, generous obedience, a changed mind, and changed behavior.

All the evidence indicated that Zaccheus was a genuine believer. Jesus saw it and recognized a heart of faith. Look again at Luke 19:9: "He, too, is a son of Abraham." That was a statement about his faith.

Zaccheus was a son of Abraham not because he was Jewish, but because he believed. Romans 2:28 says, "He is not a Jew who is one outwardly." Then what makes a true Jew? Romans 4:11 says Abraham is the father of all who believe. Galatians 3:7 says, "It is those who are of faith who are sons of Abraham." All who trust in Christ are Abraham's offspring. Thus a true son of Abraham is the same as a believer.

Salvation did not come to Zaccheus because he gave his money away, but because he became a true son of Abraham; that is, a believer. He was saved by faith, not by works. But the works were important evidence that his faith was real. Second Corinthians 5:17 says, "If anyone is in Christ, he is a new creature; the old things passed away; behold, new things have come." Genuine saving faith changes behavior, transforms thinking, and puts within a person a new heart (Ezek. 36:26). Implicit in that change of heart is a new set of desires—a desire to please God, to obey, and to reflect His righteousness. If such a change does not occur, there is no reason to think genuine salvation has taken place. If, as in the case of Zaccheus, there is evidence of faith that desires to obey, that is the mark of a true son of Abraham.

CHAPTER 7

Repentance

We observed in chapter 5 that the opening word of Jesus' first public sermon was "Repent" (Matt. 4:17). That clarion call to repentance was a ringing theme throughout His entire earthly ministry. It was how Jesus Himself described His objective: "to call . . . sinners to repentance" (Luke 5:32). He stood boldly before the stiff-necked multitudes and proclaimed, "Unless you repent, you will all likewise perish" (13:3, 5).

It's not fashionable in the twenty-first century to preach a gospel that demands repentance. But from His first message to His last, Jesus' theme was calling sinners to repentance—and this meant not only that they gained a new perspective on who He was, but also that they turned from sin and self to follow Him. The message He commands us to preach is the same: "repentance for forgiveness of sins" (Luke 24:47).

What Is Repentance?

Repentance *is* a critical element of conversion, but do not dismiss it as simply another word for believing. The Greek word for "repentance" is *metanoia*, from *meta*, "after," and *noeō*, "to understand." Literally it means "afterthought" or "change of mind," but biblically its meaning does not stop there. As *metanoia* is used in the New Testament, it *always* speaks of a change of purpose, and specifically a turning from sin. In the sense Jesus used it, repentance calls for a repudiation of the old life and a turning to God for salvation.

Such a change of purpose is what Paul had in mind when he described the repentance of the Thessalonians: "You turned to God from idols to serve a living and true God" (1 Thess. 1:9). Note three elements of repentance: a turning to God, a turning from evil, and the intent to serve God. No change of mind can be called true repentance if it does not include all three elements.

The simple but often overlooked fact is that a true change of mind will necessarily result in a change of behavior.

Repentance is not merely shame or sorrow for sin, although genuine repentance always involves an element of remorse. It is a redirection of the human will, a purposeful decision to forsake all unrighteousness and pursue righteousness instead.

Nor is repentance merely a human work. It is, like every element of redemption, a sovereignly bestowed gift of God. The early church, recognizing the authenticity of Cornelius's conversion, concluded, "Well then, God has granted to the Gentiles also the repentance that leads to life" (Acts 11:18; cf. 5:31). Paul wrote to Timothy that he should gently correct those who oppose the truth, "if perhaps God may grant them repentance leading to the knowledge of the truth" (2 Tim. 2:25). If God is the One who grants repentance, it cannot be viewed as a human work.

Above all, repentance is not a pre-salvation attempt to set one's life in order. The call to repentance is not a command to make sin right before turning to Christ in faith. Rather, it is a command to recognize one's lawlessness and hate it, to turn one's back on it and flee to Christ, embracing Him with wholehearted devotion. True repentance involves self-reproach, contrition, and rueful shame. Repentance is a fruit of godly sorrow over one's sin (2 Cor. 7:10). By definition it's incompatible with a hardened heart.

Repentance is not simply a mental activity; genuine repentance involves the intellect, emotions, and will. *Intellectually*, repentance begins with a recognition of sin—the understanding that we are sinners, that our sin is an affront to a holy God, and more precisely, that we are personally responsible for our own guilt. The repentance that leads to salvation must also include a recognition of who Christ is along with some understanding of His right to govern people's lives.

Emotionally, genuine repentance often accompanies an overwhelming sense of sorrow. This sorrow in and of itself is not repentance; one can be sorry or ashamed without being truly repentant. Judas, for example, felt remorse (Matt. 27:3), but he was not repentant. The rich young ruler went away sorrowful (19:22), but he was not repentant. Nevertheless, sorrow can lead to genuine repentance. Second Corinthians 7:10 says, "The sorrow that is according to the will of

God produces a repentance without regret." It is difficult to imagine a true repentance that does not include at least an element of contrition—not sorrow for getting caught; not sadness because of the consequences; but a sense of anguish at having sinned against God. In the Old Testament, repentance was often shown with sackcloth and ashes, the symbols of mourning (cf. Job 42:6; Jonah 3:5–6).

Volitionally, repentance involves a change of direction, a transformation of the will. Far from being only a change of mind, it constitutes a willingness—more accurately, a determination—to abandon stubborn disobedience and surrender the will to Christ. As such, genuine repentance will inevitably result in a change of behavior. The behavior change is not itself repentance, but it is the fruit repentance will certainly bear. Where there is no observable difference in conduct, there can be no confidence that repentance has taken place (Matt. 3:8; cf. 1 John 2:3–6; 3:17).

Real repentance alters one's fundamental character. It is not a one-time act. The repentance that takes place at conversion begins a progressive, lifelong process of confession (1 John 1:9). This active, continuous attitude of repentance produces the poverty of spirit, mourning, and meekness Jesus spoke of in the Beatitudes (Matt. 5:3–6). It is a mark of every true believer.

The Fruits of Repentance

When Jesus preached, "Repent, for the kingdom of heaven is at hand" (Matt. 4:17), those who heard Him understood the message. With their rich heritage in Old Testament and rabbinical teaching, His hearers would not have been confused about the meaning of repentance. They knew He was calling for far more than simply a change of mind or a new perspective on who He was. Repentance to them meant a complete surrender of their will and an inevitable change of behavior—a new way of life, not just a different opinion. They realized He was calling them to admit their sin and turn from it, to be converted, to turn around, to forsake their sin and selfishness and follow Him instead.

After all, the Jewish concept of repentance was well developed. The rabbis held that Isaiah 1:16–17 described nine activities related to repentance: "Wash yourselves, make yourselves clean; remove the evil of your deeds from My sight. Cease to do evil, learn to do good; seek justice, reprove the ruthless; defend the orphan, plead for the widow." Note carefully the progression: beginning internally with a cleansing, repentance then manifests itself in attitudes and actions.

The Old Testament was filled with rich truth about repentance. Ezekiel 33:18–19, for example, says, "When the righteous turns from his righteousness and commits iniquity, then he shall die in it. But when the wicked turns from his wickedness and practices justice and righteousness, he will live by them." Second Chronicles 7:14 is a familiar prescription for repentance: "[If] My people who are called by My name humble themselves and pray and seek My face and turn from their wicked ways, then I will hear from heaven, will forgive their sin and will heal their land." Isaiah 55:6–7 gives the Old Testament invitation to salvation, and repentance is a key element: "Seek the LORD while He may be found; call upon Him while He is near. Let the wicked forsake his way and the unrighteous man his thoughts; and let him return to the LORD, and He will have compassion on him, and to our God, for He will abundantly pardon." Jonah 3:10 says, "When God saw their deeds, that they turned from their wicked way, then God relented concerning the calamity which He had declared He would bring upon them. And He did not do it."

Look carefully at that verse from Jonah. How did God evaluate the Ninevites' repentance? By their *deeds*. It was not that He read their thoughts or heard their prayers, though an omniscient God certainly could have seen the reality of their repentance that way. But He looked for righteous works.

John the Baptist also demanded to see good deeds as proof of repentance. He preached the message of repentance even before Jesus began His ministry (cf. Matt. 3:1–2). Scripture records that when the religious hypocrites came to John for baptism, "He said to them, 'You brood of vipers, who warned you to flee from the wrath to come? Therefore bear fruit in keeping with repentance'" (Matt. 3:7–8).

What a greeting! It was a far cry from saying, "Ladies and gentlemen, here are our esteemed leaders." We do not know why they had come for baptism, but obviously their motives were wrong. Perhaps they were trying to gain favor with the people or be associated with John's popularity. Whatever their reasons, they had

not really repented, and John refused their over-
ture. He condemned them instead as religious
phonies.

Why was John so harsh? Because these
hypocrites were poisoning a whole nation
with their fatal deception. Nothing about
their behavior indicated that they had truly
repented. There is a critical lesson here: if
repentance is genuine, we can expect it to produce observable results.

What are the fruits of repentance? That is
the question the tax-gatherers asked John the
Baptist (Luke 3:10). His answer to them was,
"Collect no more than what you have been
ordered to" (v. 13). To some soldiers who asked
the same question, his response was, "Do not
take money from anyone by force, or accuse
anyone falsely, and be content with your wages"
(v. 14).

In other words, there must be a sincere
change in one's lifestyle. A person who has gen-
uinely repented will begin to mortify sinful
desires and seek to live righteously. Along with
a change of mind and attitude, true repentance
will begin to produce a change in conduct.

Radical change was also what the apostle
Paul considered proof of repentance. Note how

he described his ministry to King Agrippa: "I did not prove disobedient to the heavenly vision, but kept declaring . . . to the Gentiles, that they should repent and turn to God, *performing deeds appropriate to repentance*" (Acts 26:19–20). That true believers will show their repentance with righteous behavior was obviously a crucial element of Paul's message.

The Gospel and Repentance

Repentance has always been the foundation of the New Testament call to salvation. When Peter gave the gospel invitation at Pentecost, in the first public evangelism of the post-resurrection era, repentance was at the heart of it: "Repent, and each of you be baptized in the name of Jesus Christ for the forgiveness of your sins" (Acts 2:38).

No message that eliminates repentance can properly be called the gospel, for sinners cannot come to Jesus Christ apart from a radical change of heart, mind, and will. That demands a spiritual crisis leading to a complete turnaround and ultimately a wholesale transformation. It is the only kind of conversion Scripture recognizes.

In Matthew 21:28–31 Jesus used a parable to illustrate the hypocrisy of a profession of faith without repentance:

> "But what do you think? A man had two sons, and he came to the first and said, 'Son, go work today in the vineyard.' And he answered, 'I will not'; but afterward he regretted it and went. The man came to the second and said the same thing; and he answered, 'I will, sir'; but he did not go. Which of the two did the will of his father?"

You may wonder why Jesus did not include a third son who said, "I will" and kept his word. Perhaps it is because this story characterizes humanity, and we all fall short (cf. Rom. 3:23). Thus Jesus could describe only two kinds of religious people: those who pretend to be obedient but are actually rebels, and those who begin as rebels but repent.

Jesus told the parable for the benefit of the Pharisees, who did not view themselves as sinful and disobedient. When He asked them which son did the will of his father, they correctly answered, "The first" (Matt. 21:31). In admitting that, they condemned themselves for their own hypocrisy.

How Jesus' rebuke must have stung them! "Truly I say to you that the tax collectors and prostitutes will get into the kingdom of God before you" (v. 31). The Pharisees lived under the delusion that God approved of them because they made a great show of their religion. The problem was that it was only a show. They were like the son who said he would obey but did not. Their claim that they loved God and kept His law amounted to nothing. Those Pharisees were like many today who say they believe in Jesus but refuse to obey Him. Their profession of faith is hollow. Unless they repent, they will perish.

Tax collectors and prostitutes have an easier time than Pharisees getting into the kingdom because they are more likely to recognize their sin and repent of it. Even the worst of sins will not keep a sinner out of heaven if he or she repents. On the other hand, even the most impressive Pharisee who shelters his sin and refuses to acknowledge or repent of it will find himself shut out of the kingdom. There is no salvation apart from the repentance that renounces sin.

There are many today who hear the truth of Christ and immediately respond as did the son who said he would obey but did not. Their positive response to Jesus will not save them. The fruit of their lives shows they have never truly repented.

On the other hand, there are many who turn their backs on sin, unbelief, and disobedience, and embrace Christ with a faith that obeys. Theirs is true repentance, manifested by the righteousness it produces. They are the truly righteous (1 Peter 4:18).

CHAPTER 8

Faith

Just as I am, without one plea
But that Thy blood was shed for me,
And that Thou bidd'st me come to Thee,
O Lamb of God, I come! I come!

That stanza, penned by Charlotte Elliot in the nineteenth century, has probably been used as background for the evangelistic invitation more than any other hymn in history. The thought these words convey is a glorious biblical reality: sinners may come to Christ just as they are—solely on the basis of repentant faith—and He will save them. The Lord's own wonderful promise is in John 3:16: "For God so loved the world, that He gave His only begotten Son, that *whoever* believes in Him shall not perish, but have eternal life." Later He added, "The one who comes to Me I will certainly not cast out" (John 6:37).

The erosion of the gospel in our day has given this truth an insidious twist. The language of the modern message sounds vaguely similar to "Just as I Am," but the difference in meaning is profound. Sinners today hear not only that Christ will receive them as they are, but also that He will let them stay that way! Many erroneously believe they can come to Christ, receive absolution and immortality, then walk away to continue living life as they please according to the desires of their own flesh.

A few years ago leaders of a Christian ministry for young people asked me to preview a training film they produced. The subject was evangelism, and the film instructed youth workers not to tell unsaved young people they must obey Christ, give Him their hearts, surrender their lives, repent of their sins, submit to His lordship, or follow Him. Telling the unsaved they must do those things confuses the gospel message, the film said. It advocated giving only the objective facts about Jesus' death (making no mention of the resurrection), and pressing on them the need to believe. The film concluded that the sum total of saving faith is understanding and accepting the facts of the gospel.

I once spoke at a Bible conference where a well-known Bible teacher brought a message on salvation. He suggested that telling unsaved people they must surrender to Christ is the same as preaching works. He defined salvation as the unconditional gift of everlasting life given to people who believe the facts about Christ, *whether they choose to obey Him or not*. One of his main points was that salvation may or may not alter a person's behavior. Transformed conduct is certainly desirable, he said, but even if no change in lifestyle occurs, the one who has believed the facts of the gospel can rest in the certainty of heaven.

Multitudes approach Christ on those terms. Thinking He will not confront their sin, they respond eagerly—but with no sense of the severity of their guilt before God and with no desire to be freed from sin's bondage. They have been deceived by a corrupted gospel. They have been told that faith alone will save them, but they neither understand nor possess real faith. The "faith" they are relying on is only a superficial nod of agreement rather than a wholehearted embrace of the truth. It is not saving faith.

Eternal Life from Dead Faith?

Scripture expressly deals with that brand of non-redemptive, notional "faith." James 2:14–17 says faith without works is dead and cannot save. James describes spurious faith as pure hypocrisy (v. 16), mere cognitive assent (v. 19), devoid of any verifying works (vv. 17–18)—no different from the demons' belief (v. 19). Obviously there is more to saving faith than merely conceding a set of facts. Faith without works is useless (v. 20).

Today's popular approaches to evangelism often foster and encourage precisely that kind of barren faith. The gospel appeal is tacked onto a wholly inadequate explanation of what it means to believe. Because the modern definition of faith eliminates repentance, it evacuates the moral significance of believing; it obviates the work of God in the sinner's heart; it makes an ongoing trust in the Lord optional. Christians who adjust the gospel in that fashion typically insist they are safeguarding the truth that salvation is by faith alone. Ironically, they have turned faith itself into a wholly human work. Such "faith" is a fragile, fleshly, cursory presumption that cannot endure.

Scripture expressly refutes the notion that a person can truly believe at the moment of salvation and then later abandon the faith. Professing Christians do sometimes abandon the faith, of course. But speaking of such people, the apostle John wrote, "They went out from us, but they were not really of us; for if they had been of us, they would have remained with us; but they went out, so that it would be shown that they all are not of us" (1 John 2:19).

Paul's words in 2 Timothy 2:12 also speak powerfully to this issue: "If we endure, we shall also reign with Him; if we deny Him, He also will deny us." Endurance is the mark of those who will reign with Christ in His kingdom. Clearly, enduring is a characteristic of true believers, while disloyalty and defection reveal a heart of unbelief. Those who deny Christ, He will deny. Paul goes on to say, "If we are faithless, He remains faithful; for He cannot deny Himself" (v. 13). Thus God's faithfulness is a blessed comfort to loyal, abiding believers but a frightening warning to false professors (cf. John 3:17–18).

Faith as Scripture Describes It

We have seen already that repentance is granted by God; it is not a human work (Acts 11:18;

2 Tim. 2:25). Likewise, faith is a supernatural gift of God. Ephesians 2:8–9 is a familiar passage: "By grace you have been saved through faith; and that not of yourselves, it is the gift of God; not as a result of works, so that no one may boast." What is "the gift of God" Paul speaks of? The answer is not simple, because the phrase "that not of yourselves" has no clear antecedent. The Greek pronoun translated "that" is neuter, and the word for "faith" is feminine. The antecedent of "that," it would seem, cannot be the word *faith*. "That" might refer to the act of believing, employing an antecedent that is not stated but understood. It is also possible that Paul had in mind the entire process—grace, faith, and salvation—as the gift of God. Both possibilities certainly are in keeping with the context: "Even when we were dead in our transgressions, [God] made us alive together with Christ (by grace you have been saved)" (v. 5). Spiritually dead, we were helpless until God intervened to quicken us. Faith is an integral part of the "gift" His grace bestowed on us.

Consistently the Scriptures teach that faith is not conjured up by the human will but is a sovereignly granted gift of God. Jesus said, "No one can come to Me unless the Father who sent

Me draws him" (John 6:44). And "No one can come to Me unless it has been granted him from the Father" (v. 65). Acts 3:16 speaks of "the faith which comes through Him." Philippians 1:29 says, "To you it has been granted for Christ's sake . . . to believe in Him." And Peter wrote to fellow believers as "those who have received a faith of the same kind as ours" (2 Peter 1:1).

How do we know that faith is God's gift? Left to ourselves, no one would ever believe: "There is none who understands, there is none who seeks for God" (Rom. 3:11). "So then it does not depend on the man who wills or the man who runs, but on God who has mercy" (Rom. 9:16). God draws the sinner to Christ and gives the ability to believe. Without that divinely generated faith, one cannot understand and approach the Savior. "A natural man does not accept the things of the Spirit of God, for they are foolishness to him; and he cannot understand them, because they are spiritually appraised" (1 Cor. 2:14). That is precisely why when Peter affirmed his faith in Christ as the Son of God, Jesus told him, "Blessed are you, Simon Barjona, because flesh and blood did not reveal this to you, but My Father who is in heaven" (Matt. 16:17). Faith is graciously given to believers by God Himself.

As a divine gift, faith is neither transient nor impotent. It has an abiding quality that guarantees it will endure to the end. The familiar words of Habakkuk 2:4, "The righteous will live by his faith" (cf. Rom. 1:17; Gal. 3:11; Heb. 10:38), speak not of a momentary act of believing, but of a living, enduring trust in God. Hebrews 3:14 emphasizes the permanence of genuine faith. Its very durability is proof of its reality: "We have become partakers of Christ, if we hold fast the beginning of our assurance firm until the end." The faith God gives can never evaporate. And the work of salvation cannot ultimately be thwarted. In Philippians 1:6 Paul wrote, "I am confident of this very thing, that He who began a good work in you will perfect it until the day of Christ Jesus" (cf. 1 Cor. 1:8; Col. 1:22–23).

The faith God graciously supplies produces both the volition and the ability to comply with His will (cf. Phil. 2:13: "God . . . is at work in you, both to will and to work for His good pleasure"). Thus faith is inseparable from obedience, and the person who has believed will *yearn* to obey. Because we retain the vestiges of sinful flesh, no one will obey perfectly (cf. 2 Cor. 7:1; 1 Thess. 3:10), but the desire to do the will of God will be ever present in true believers (cf. Rom. 7:18).

That is why faith and obedience are so closely linked throughout Scripture.

A concept of faith not producing surrender of the will corrupts the message of salvation. Paul spoke of the gospel as something to be obeyed (Rom. 10:16 KJV; 2 Thess. 1:8). Here is how he characterized conversion: "Though you were slaves of sin, you became obedient from the heart" (Rom. 6:17). The result he sought in his ministry of evangelism was "obedience . . . by word and deed" (15:18). And he wrote repeatedly of "the obedience of faith" (1:5; 16:26).

Clearly, the biblical concept of faith is inseparable from obedience. "Believe" is treated as if it were synonymous with "obey" in John 3:36: "He who believes in the Son has eternal life; but he who does not obey the Son will not see life." Acts 6:7 shows how salvation was understood in the early church: "A great many . . . were becoming obedient to the faith." Obedience is so closely related to saving faith that Hebrews 5:9 uses it as a synonym: "Having been made perfect, He became to all those who obey Him the source of eternal salvation." Hebrews 11, the great treatise on faith, presents obedience and faith as inseparable: "By faith Abraham . . . obeyed" (v. 8)—and not just Abraham. All the heroes of faith listed in Hebrews 11 showed their faith by obedience.

Obedience is the inevitable manifestation of true faith. Paul recognized this when he wrote to Titus about "those who are defiled and unbelieving . . . .They profess to know God, but by their deeds they deny Him" (Titus 1:15–16). To Paul, their perpetual disobedience proved their disbelief. Their actions denied God more loudly than their words proclaimed Him. This is characteristic of unbelief, not faith, for true faith always embodies righteous works. As the Reformers were fond of saying, we are justified by faith alone, but justifying faith is never alone. True faith is manifest only in obedience.

Faith and faithfulness were not substantially different concepts to the first-century Christian. In fact, the same word is translated both ways in our English Bibles. The faithful (believing) are also faithful (obedient). Fidelity, constancy, and trust are all inherent in the biblical description of faith. Righteous living is therefore an inevitable by-product of real faith (Rom. 10:10).

Of course, that is not to say that faith results in anything like sinless perfection. All true believers understand the plea of the demon-possessed boy's father, "I do believe; help my unbelief" (Mark 9:24). Those who believe *will* desire to obey, however imperfectly they may follow through at times. So-called "faith" in God that does not produce this yearning to submit to His will is not faith at all. The state of mind that refuses obedience is pure and simple unbelief.

Faith as Jesus Presented It

The Beatitudes (Matt. 5:3–12) reveal the character of true faith as well as any passage of Scripture I know. These traits—poverty of spirit, hunger and thirst for righteousness, purity of heart, and so on—are not just an unobtainable legal standard. These are characteristics common to all who believe. The first of the Beatitudes leaves no doubt about whom the Lord is speaking: "Blessed are the poor in spirit, *for theirs is the kingdom of heaven*" (Matt. 5:3). He is describing redeemed people, those who have believed, those who are part of the kingdom. Here is what their faith is like.

Its foundational characteristic is humility—a poverty of spirit, a brokenness that acknowledges spiritual bankruptcy. Genuine believers see themselves as sinners; they know they have nothing to offer God that will buy His favor. That is why they mourn (v. 4), with the sorrow that accompanies true repentance. It crushes the believer into meekness (v. 5). He hungers and thirsts for righteousness (v. 6). As the Lord satisfies that hunger, He makes the believing one merciful (v. 6), pure in heart (v. 7), and a peacemaker (v. 9). The believer is ultimately persecuted and reviled for righteousness' sake (v. 10).

That is Jesus' description of the genuine believer. Each of the characteristics He names—starting with humility and reaching fruition in obedience—is a consequence of true faith. And note that the obedience of faith is more than external; it issues from the heart. That is one reason the righteousness of the redeemed is greater than the righteousness of the scribes and Pharisees (v. 20): it is not just superficial. Jesus goes on to characterize true righteousness—the righteousness that is born of faith (cf. Rom. 10:6)—as obedience not just to the letter of the law, but to the spirit of the law as well (Matt. 5:21–48). This kind of righteousness does not merely avoid acts of adultery; it goes so far as to avoid adulterous thoughts. It eschews hatred the same as murder.

If you see that God's standard is higher than you can possibly attain, you are on the road to the blessedness Jesus spoke of in the Beatitudes. It begins with the humility that grows out of a sense of utter spiritual poverty, the knowledge that we are poor in spirit. And it consummates inevitably in righteous obedience. Those are characteristics of a supernatural life. They are impossible apart from faith, and it is impossible that someone with true faith might be utterly lacking these characteristics that are common to everyone in the kingdom (Matt. 5:3).

When Jesus wanted to illustrate the character of saving faith, He took a little child, stood him in the midst of the disciples, and said, "Truly I say to you, unless you are converted and become like children, you will not enter the kingdom of heaven" (Matt. 18:3). A child was the perfect picture of obedient humility, an object lesson about saving faith.

Jesus used this illustration to teach that if we insist on retaining the privileges of adulthood—if we want to be our own boss, do our own thing, govern our own lives—we cannot enter into the kingdom of heaven. But if we are willing to come on the basis of childlike faith and receive salvation with the humility of a child, with a willingness to surrender to Christ's authority, then we are coming with the right attitude.

Jesus said, "My sheep hear My voice, and I know them, and they *follow* Me; and I give eternal life to them, and they will never perish" (John 10:27–28). Who are the true sheep? The ones who follow. Who are the ones who follow? The ones who are given eternal life.

Faith obeys. Unbelief rebels. Christians can and do fall into sin, of course. But the long-term direction of one's life will reveal whether that person is a believer or an unbeliever.

Merely knowing and affirming facts apart from obedience to the truth is not believing in the biblical sense. Those who cling to the memory of a one-time decision of "faith" but lack any evidence of the outworking of faith had better heed the clear and solemn warning of Scripture: "He who does not obey the Son will not see life, but the wrath of God abides on him" (John 3:36).

CHAPTER 9

Justification

Without a doubt, the most unsettling aspect of Jesus' Sermon on the Mount was this shocking statement: "Therefore you are to be perfect, as your heavenly Father is perfect" (Matt. 5:48).

If the gauge of righteousness is absolute perfection, what hope is there for anyone?

The people listening to Jesus that day believed that the scribes and Pharisees were the embodiment of the highest human righteousness. And in a sense they were—they held to the strictest imaginable legalistic standards. Here is how the apostle Paul chronicled his life as a Pharisee: "Circumcised the eighth day, of the nation of Israel, of the tribe of Benjamin, a Hebrew of Hebrews; as to the Law, a Pharisee;

as to zeal, a persecutor of the church; as to the righteousness which is in the Law, found blameless" (Phil. 3:5–6). The Pharisees fasted, prayed, abstained from questionable practices, paid tithes, gave alms, memorized Scripture—and even devised their own rigid laws that went beyond what God had commanded in Scripture.

Yet Jesus said, "Unless your righteousness *surpasses* that of the scribes and Pharisees, you will not enter the kingdom of heaven" (Matt. 5:20). If you believe that establishes an impossible standard, you have understood the message.

Remember the rich young ruler? He was a Pharisee who evidently believed he had kept the law as completely as humanly possible. After he walked away unbelieving, Jesus told His disciples, "It is hard for a rich man to enter the kingdom of heaven" (Matt. 19:23). What was their response? Astonished, they asked Him, "Then who can be saved?" (v. 25).

Jesus' reply was, "With people this is impossible, but with God all things are possible" (v. 26).

Salvation is impossible for sinful humanity. We have no redeeming resources of our own. We cannot atone for our sins. We cannot even believe without God's sovereign enablement (John 6:44, 65); we cannot conjure up faith out of the human will. And we certainly cannot live up to God's standard of perfect righteousness.

In the sixteenth century, Martin Luther sat in the tower of the Black Cloister in Wittenberg, meditating on the perfect righteousness of God. Although he was the most scrupulous of monks, attending confession for hours each day, seeking forgiveness for the minutest of sins, he realized that the standard of perfect righteousness was absolutely unattainable. He thought of divine righteousness as an unrelenting, unforgiving, avenging wrath and believed his state was hopeless.

Then while reading the Bible, he came to understand that the righteousness the apostle Paul celebrated so joyfully is a perfect righteousness that is imputed to us, not the flawed and worthless "righteousness" we earn for ourselves. In Paul's words, it was "not . . . a righteousness of my own derived from the Law, but that which is through faith in Christ, the righteousness which comes from God on the basis of faith" (Phil. 3:9).

The remedy Luther found was the doctrine of justification by faith. His discovery launched the Reformation and put an end to the Dark

Ages. What Luther came to realize is that God's righteousness, revealed in the gospel, is reckoned in full to the account of everyone who turns to Christ in repentant faith. God's own righteousness thus becomes the ground on which believers stand before Him.

This doctrine of justification is most fully expounded by the apostle Paul. The book of Romans in particular includes a lengthy treatise on justification, in which Paul demonstrates that as far back as Genesis, God graciously saved people by reckoning His righteousness to them because of their faith. No one has ever been saved through the merit system—salvation has been available only by grace through faith ever since our first parents fell. Abraham is the prime example of this: "Abraham believed God, and it was credited to him as righteousness" (Rom. 4:3).

What Is Justification?

During His earthly ministry, Jesus rarely used the word *justification*. Nevertheless, justification by faith was the underlying theme of the message He preached. Look again at the parable of the Pharisee and the publican:

He also told this parable to some people who trusted in themselves that they were righteous, and viewed others with contempt: "Two men went up into the temple to pray, one a Pharisee and the other a tax collector. The Pharisee stood and was praying this to himself, 'God, I thank You that I am not like other people: swindlers, unjust, adulterers, or even like this tax collector. I fast twice a week; I pay tithes of all that I get.' But the tax collector, standing some distance away, was even unwilling to lift up his eyes to heaven, but was beating his breast, saying, 'God, be merciful to me, the sinner!'" (Luke 18:9–13).

Jesus must have drawn gasps from the Pharisees when He punctuated His story with this pronouncement: "I tell you, this man [the tax collector] went to his house *justified* rather than the other [the Pharisee]; for everyone who exalts himself will be humbled, but he who humbles himself will be exalted" (v. 14).

The parable reveals that justification is instantaneous. The repentant tax collector "went to his house justified"; that is, there was no time lapse—no works of penance, no ritual, no sacrament, no confessional exercise, no meritorious deeds he needed to do before he could be whole in God's eyes. Everything had already been done on his behalf. He was justified by faith on the spot.

Here our Lord simply states the *fact* of justification; He does not explain the *theology* of it. Still, the parable is an ideal portrait of justification by faith, in perfect harmony with the doctrine that Paul would later articulate so clearly in Romans 3–5.

Justification may be defined as an act of God whereby He imputes to a believing sinner the full and perfect righteousness of Christ, forgiving the sinner of all unrighteousness, declaring him or her perfectly righteous in God's sight, thus delivering the believer from all condemnation. That definition contains several elements: imputed righteousness, forgiveness of sins, a new standing before God, and a reversal of God's wrath. Those all indicate that justification is a legal verdict. It is a forensic reality that takes place in the court of God, not in the heart of the sinner. In other words, justification is an instantaneous change of one's standing before God, not a gradual transformation that takes place within the one who is justified.

There are two serious errors to avoid in the

matter of justification. First, do not confuse justification with sanctification. Roman Catholic theology makes this error. *Sanctification* is the work of God whereby He sets the believer apart from sin. Sanctification is a practical reality, not simply a legal declaration. Sanctification involves a change in the sinner's character, not just a new standing before God. By including sanctification as an aspect of justification, Catholic theology renders instantaneous justification impossible. Worse, this view substitutes the believer's own imperfect righteousness in place of Christ's unblemished righteousness, as the basis of justification.

There is a second, equally dangerous, error: do not separate justification and sanctification so radically that you allow for one without the other. This is the error of *antinomianism*. God will not justify those He does not sanctify. God does not offer justification as a stand-alone means of salvation. Election, regeneration, faith, justification, sanctification, and even glorification are all integral facets of God's saving work: "Whom He foreknew, He also predestined to become conformed to the image of His Son [sanctification] . . . . and these whom He predestined, He also called; and these whom He called, He also justified; and these whom He justified, He also glorified" (Rom. 8:29–30). Justification cannot be isolated and made to represent the sum of God's saving work. Yet that is exactly the error that is rampant in contemporary theology.

Imputed Righteousness

The cornerstone of justification is the reckoning of righteousness to the believer's account. This is the truth that sets Christian doctrine apart from every form of false religion. We call it "imputed righteousness." Apart from it, salvation is utterly impossible.

Sin defiles us. The apostle James wrote, "Whoever keeps the whole law and yet stumbles in one point, he has become guilty of all" (James 2:10). No amount of doing good can make up for even one sin. The person who has sinned owes an impossible debt.

Moreover, a righteous God cannot simply overlook sin or act as if it never occurred. There must be atonement for sin. Law demands a penalty for sin, and it is a penalty that must be paid: "The wages of sin is death" (Rom. 6:23).

Yet atonement alone does not fully solve the problem. If it were somehow possible for sinners to atone for their sins and obtain forgiveness, they would still stand before God without merit. Although their guilt would be erased, they would still lack the perfect righteousness God requires (Matt. 5:20, 48).

Imputed righteousness solves the dilemma. Christ made atonement by shedding His own blood on the cross. That provides forgiveness. And just as our sins were put to His account when He bore them on the cross, so now His righteousness is reckoned as our own. His perfect righteousness thus becomes the ground on which we stand before God.

This is a crucial point on which Protestants have historically been in full agreement: sinners are not justified because of some good thing in them; God can declare them righteous because He first imputes to them the perfect righteousness of Christ. We stand before God as if we were perfectly just. Judicially, the Father views us as if our righteousness were on the same lofty plane as His Son's!

Again, this is owing to no good thing in us— not even God's sanctifying or regenerating work in our hearts. Justification is possible exclusively through the imputed righteousness of Christ: "To the one who does not work, but believes in Him who justifies the ungodly, *his faith is credited as righteousness*" (Rom. 4:5). "Those who receive the abundance of grace and of *the gift of righteousness* will reign in life through the One, Jesus Christ" (5:17). "Through the obedience of the One the many will be made [declared] righteous" (v. 19). "Now apart from the Law the righteousness of God has been manifested, being witnessed by the Law and the Prophets, even *the righteousness of God through faith in Jesus Christ for all those who believe*" (3:21–22). "He made Him who knew no sin to be sin on our behalf, that we might become the righteousness of God in Him" (2 Cor. 5:21). "Not having a righteousness of my own derived from the Law, but that which is through faith in Christ, *the righteousness which comes from God on the basis of faith*" (Phil. 3:9).

Forgiveness of Sins

Justification also guarantees the forgiveness and remission of sins. That may seem obvious from the meaning of the word. Yet it is not the kind of forgiveness that merely excuses or disregards wrongdoing. As noted, if God simply ignored sins, He would compromise His own holiness. Instead, the penalty sin demands was fully paid in the death of Christ. We are therefore "justified as a gift by His grace through the redemption which is in Christ Jesus; whom God displayed publicly as a propitiation in His blood through faith. This was to demonstrate His righteousness . . . *that He would be just and the justifier of the one who has faith in Jesus*" (Rom. 3:24–26).

God can justify without besmirching His own righteousness because Christ made *propitiation*. That is a technical term describing the reconciliation of God to the sinner. Christ atoned for our sins; God is therefore propitiated. In other words, He is kindly disposed to us and eager to forgive. The enmity has been removed. The full price was paid, so God can receive believing sinners with no taint on His own righteousness.

A New Standing

"This man went to his house justified" (Luke 18:14) describes the tax-gatherer's standing before God. It is not difficult to imagine the Pharisees' anger when Jesus related this story. In essence He was telling them that a pathetic publican in abject repentance was more acceptable to God than they were.

The reason for this is quite simple: they "trusted *in themselves* that they were righteous" (v. 9). Likewise, the Pharisee in the parable was seeking justification on the basis of his own righteousness: "I am not like other people: swindlers, unjust, adulterers, or even like this tax collector. I fast twice a week; I pay tithes of all that I get" (vv. 11–12). We commonly call such people *self*-righteous. Have you ever considered why? It is because they assume they have ample righteousness of their own and do not see the need for imputed righteousness.

But the tax-gatherer was under no such delusion. All he could do was repent and plead for mercy. And so perfect righteousness was imputed to his account. Forever thereafter he stood before God fully justified.

Reversal of God's Wrath

Justification is the polar opposite of condemnation. One of the most blessed of all biblical truths is found in Romans 8:1: "There is now no

condemnation for those who are in Christ Jesus."
Justification by faith is what makes that possible.
If God's demeanor toward us were determined
by our own behavior, no one could escape His
wrath; for all of us are wretched sinners—even
the most mature saint in Christ (cf. Rom. 7:24).
But we who are in Christ need not fear condemnation; we have been justified.

What do you suppose would have become
of the tax-gatherer in Jesus' parable? Do you
think he would have continued praying in fear
and anguish week after week? Certainly not.
Like Matthew and Zaccheus, two real-life tax-
gatherers we have already met, this man would
have discovered that justification offers the only
possible relief from the guilt of sin. We can be
certain that his life would not have continued
as before.

Justification and the Life of the Believer

We noted above that antinomianism is the
notion of justification apart from sanctification.
Luther himself coined the term, for already in
his lifetime, some were beginning to corrupt

the doctrine he had rediscovered, claiming that justification by faith rendered unnecessary the preaching of the law, obedience to the law, or sanctification as evidence of justification.

Luther's remedy for antinomianism was preaching the law of God, because he rightly understood that those who comfort themselves with the promise of justification while living in wanton unrighteousness are thereby shown that theirs is a false security.

Does justification by faith make way for licentious living? Not if the doctrine is properly understood. Paul anticipated the antinomian argument: "What shall we say then? Are we to continue in sin so that grace may increase?" (Rom. 6:1). "What then? Shall we sin because we are not under law but under grace? May it never be!" (v. 15). Romans 6 is Paul's rebuttal to antinomianism. He argues that our union with Christ guarantees we shall no longer be slaves of sin: "Our old self was crucified with Him, in order that our body of sin might be done away with, so that we would no longer be slaves to sin; for he who has died is freed from sin" (vv. 6–7).

The work of God in salvation does not stop with justification. God does not declare sinners righteous only to abandon them to their own energies. The glorious justification our Lord spoke of is only the beginning of the abundant life He promised (cf. John 10:10). "He who believes in Me, as the Scripture said, 'From his innermost being will flow rivers of living water'" (John 7:38). The full redemption He promised and purchased for His people brings not only justification, but also sanctification, union with Him, the indwelling Holy Spirit, and an eternity of blessing. It is not merely a one-time legal transaction.

But a one-time legal transaction—justification—is the turning point. It is what moves us into a new relationship with God so that we can walk in the light as He is in the light (cf. 1 John 1:7). It is what brings peace with God in place of enmity (Rom. 5:1). It is what makes us heirs according to the hope of eternal life (Titus 3:7). It is the heart of all God's work on our behalf, beginning with His foreknowledge before the foundation of the world and carrying on to our final glorification with Him (Rom. 8:29–30).

CHAPTER 10

The Cost of Discipleship

In previous chapters we have touched on Jesus' call to discipleship. Here we will examine it more closely. Let me say again unequivocally that Jesus' summons to deny self and follow Him was an invitation to salvation, not an offer of a "higher life" or a second step of faith following salvation. The contemporary teaching that separates discipleship from salvation springs from ideas that are foreign to Scripture.

Every Christian is a disciple. In fact, the Lord's Great Commission was to go into all the world and "make disciples . . . teaching them to observe all that I commanded you" (Matt. 28:19–20).

That means the mission of the church, and the goal of evangelism, is to make disciples. Disciples are people who believe, those whose faith motivates them to obey all Jesus commanded. The word *disciple* is used consistently as a synonym for *believer* throughout the book of Acts (6:1, 2, 7; 11:26; 14:20, 22; 15:10). Any distinction between the two words is purely artificial. Though introduced by sincere and well-meaning men, it has given birth to a theology of superficial faith that disposes of the hard demands of Jesus.

When Jesus called disciples, He carefully instructed them about the cost of following Him. Half-hearted people who were not willing to make the commitment did not respond. Thus He turned away anyone who was reluctant to pay the price—such as the rich young ruler. He warned all who thought of becoming disciples to count the cost carefully. "Which one of you, when he wants to build a tower, does not first sit down and calculate the cost to see if he has enough to complete it? Otherwise, when he has laid a foundation and is not able to finish, all who observe it begin to ridicule him, saying, 'This man began to build and was not able to finish'" (Luke 14:28–30).

A Christian is not one who simply buys

"fire insurance," who "accepts Christ" just to escape hell. As we have seen repeatedly, true believers' faith expresses itself in submission and obedience. Christians follow Christ. They are committed unquestionably to Christ as Lord and Savior. They desire to please God. They are humble, meek learners. When they fail, they seek forgiveness and move forward. That is their spirit and their direction.

The call to Christian discipleship explicitly demands just that kind of total dedication. It is full commitment, with nothing knowingly or deliberately held back. No one can come to Christ on any other terms. Those who think they can simply affirm a list of gospel facts and continue to live any way they please should examine themselves to see if they are really in the faith (2 Cor. 13:5).

In Matthew 10:32–39, Jesus challenged His disciples, saying:

> Everyone who confesses Me before men, I will also confess him before My Father who is in heaven. But whoever denies Me before men, I will also deny him before My Father who is in heaven . . . . He who loves father or mother more

than Me is not worthy of Me; and he who loves son or daughter more than Me is not worthy of Me. And he who does not take his cross and follow after Me is not worthy of Me. He who has found his life will lose it, and he who has lost his life for My sake will find it.

Our Lord gave no more definitive statement on discipleship than that. He spells out in the clearest possible language the cost of discipleship. The words are addressed to the Twelve in particular, but they are principles of discipleship applicable to us all. Matthew 10:24 says, "A disciple is not above his teacher." *A disciple* here means any disciple, and the words that follow, to the end of the chapter, apply to discipleship in general.

Those who see disciples as a separate class of more dedicated believers will point out that the Twelve—or at least eleven of them—were already believers in Christ and thus did not need instruction on what it means to come to Christ with saving faith. It is true that most of the disciples were undoubtedly already born again, but that does not negate the impact of these words for them. The fact is, these men were already called *disciples*, too (Matt. 10:1). This was not an invitation to a higher kind of relationship, but a reminder of what had already been established when they believed. Our Lord was continuing to teach them the meaning of faith and salvation, and constantly reminding them of the commitment they had made when they chose to follow Him.

These words apply to you and me as well. Luke 14:25–35 contains similar words—in even stronger language—which Jesus spoke not just to the Twelve, but to the multitudes who came to hear Him.

Matthew 10:2 refers to the Twelve as "apostles." That means "sent ones." Their basic training being complete, Jesus sent them out to preach. In this parting charge to them, however, He uses the word *disciple*, not *apostle*. His words apply to every disciple, serving as a signpost to every potential follower of Jesus.

Confessing Christ before Others

Verses 32–33 in Matthew 10 are reminiscent of the awesome judgment scene in Matthew 7:21–23: "Everyone who confesses Me before men, I will also confess him before My Father who is in heaven. But whoever denies Me before men, I will also deny him before My Father who is in heaven." Does that mean confession before others is a condition of becoming a true Christian? No, but it means that a characteristic of every genuine believer is that he or she *will* profess faith in Christ unreservedly. Paul wrote, "I am not ashamed of the gospel, for it is the power of God for salvation" (Rom. 1:16).

The heart of real discipleship is a commitment to be like Jesus Christ. That means both acting as He did and being willing to accept the same treatment. It means facing a world that is hostile to Him and doing it fearlessly. It means confessing before others that Jesus is Lord and being confident that He will also speak on our behalf before the Father.

"Confess" means to affirm, to acknowledge, to agree. It is a statement of identification, faith, confidence, and trust. One can confess Christ with the mouth, as Romans 10:9 says, and also confess Him through righteous behavior, as Titus 1:16 implies. We are to confess Christ "before men." This emphasizes the public character of the confession, and its meaning cannot be avoided. In Romans 10:10 we read, "With the heart a person believes, resulting in righteous-ness, and with the mouth he confesses, resulting in salvation." If the heart truly believes, the mouth will be eager to confess. Confession is not merely a human work; it is prompted and ener-gized by God, subsequent to the act of believing but inseparable from it. Again, confession is a characteristic of true faith; it is not an additional condition of salvation.

First John 4:15 says, "Whoever confesses that Jesus is the Son of God, God abides in him, and he in God." What is the mark of a true Christian? He confesses Jesus as the Son of God.

This does not mean a disciple will stand up for the Lord on every occasion. Peter denied the Lord three times on the night He was betrayed. Then there was Timothy, perhaps the finest of Paul's disciples, pastor of the church at Ephesus. This dedicated young man with such marvelous pastoral gifts was a model disciple. But he may have experienced a temporary spiritual malfunc-tion, or perhaps he was susceptible to fear. Paul had to write to him, "Do not be ashamed of the testimony of our Lord" (2 Tim. 1:8).

A moment of failure does not invalidate a dis-ciple's credentials. We have all failed to confess Christ before others more often than we would like to admit. But if we are true disciples, we will not purposely and in a calculated way keep our faith hidden from everyone all the time. Even Joseph of Arimathea, whom the apostle John called a "secret disciple," had the boldness to go to Governor Pilate after the crucifixion and ask for the body of Jesus (John 19:38).

Christ says He will confess us before the Father in heaven (Matt. 10:32). What does that mean? Christ will say on the day of judgment, "This one belongs to Me." He will affirm His loyalty to those who have affirmed their loyalty to Him. The other side of it is also stated: "But whoever denies Me before men, I will also deny him before My Father who is in heaven" (v. 33). This does not speak primarily of open rejecters— people who would deny Christ flagrantly, have nothing to do with Him, despise Him, speak against Him, or blaspheme His name. The truth certainly applies to people like that, but our Lord is talking specifically about false disciples, people who claim to be Christians but are not.

When put to the test, they consistently deny the Lord, either by their silence, by their actions, or by their words. In fact, the idea here encompasses all those things. It speaks of someone whose entire life is a denial of Christ.

He may claim to believe, but everything about his way of living exudes denial (cf. Titus 1:16). Churches are filled with such people, masquerading as disciples but routinely denying the Lord in some very disturbing ways. Christ will deny them before God (Matt. 10:33).

Matthew 25:31–46 details what will happen in the judgment. Specifically, this passage describes the separation of the sheep and goats at the end of the Tribulation, at the judgment of the nations (v. 32). But its principle applies to individuals in every phase of God's judgment. Here the Lord puts the sheep (those who have confessed Him) on His right hand, and the goats (those who have denied Him) on His left (v. 33), and ushers the sheep into the kingdom. These are the righteous people who have confessed Him. How do we know? He says, "I was hungry, and you gave Me something to eat; I was thirsty, and you gave Me something to drink; I was a stranger, and you invited Me in; naked, and you clothed Me; I was sick, and you visited Me; I was in prison, and you came to Me" (vv. 35–36). Once again, we see that the pattern of their lives reveals the reality of their claim to know Christ. Those who fail to live in a way that is consistent with faith in Christ are sent to eternal punishment (v. 46).

Getting the Priorities Straight

A second hallmark of a true disciple is loving Christ even more than one's own family (Matt. 10:35–37). Verse 37 in particular is very strong: "He who loves father or mother more than Me is not worthy of Me; and he who loves son or daughter more than Me is not worthy of Me."

If you think that is forceful, look at the parallel passage in Luke 14:26–27: "If anyone comes to Me, and does not hate his own father and mother and wife and children and brothers and sisters, yes, and even his own life, he cannot be My disciple."

To be a disciple, must we literally hate our families? Obviously this does not call for hatred in any sense that would violate the clear commandments of God, such as, "Honor your father and your mother" (Ex. 20:12), and, "Husbands, love your wives" (Eph. 5:25). The key to this passage is the phrase "yes, and even his own life" (Luke 14:26). The Lord is saying we must be unquestioningly loyal to Him, even above our families—and especially above ourselves. Scripture teaches we are to deny self (Matt. 16:24), consider ourselves dead (Rom. 6:11), lay the old self aside (Eph. 4:22)—to treat the selfish aspect of our beings with the utmost contempt (cf. 1 Cor. 9:27). That is the same attitude we are to have toward our earthly possessions and even toward our families.

Why is this language so severe? Why does Christ use such offensive terms? Because He is as eager to drive the uncommitted away as He is to draw true disciples to Himself. He does not want halfhearted people to be deceived into thinking they are in the kingdom. Unless He is honored as Lord, He has not been given His rightful place.

Taking Up the Cross

Those who are not willing to lose their lives for Christ are not worthy of Him (Matt. 10:38). They cannot be His disciples (Luke 14:27). These statements cannot be made to accommodate the casual approach to conversion that is in vogue in our generation. Jesus is not asking people to add Him to the milieu of their lives. He wants disciples willing to forsake *everything*. This calls for full-scale self-denial—even willingness to die for His sake if necessary.

When Matthew 10:38 says, "He who does not take his cross and follow after Me is not worthy of Me," it does not mean bearing the "cross" of a difficult situation, a chronic disease, or a nagging spouse. I have heard devotional sermons spiritualizing the cross to mean everything from a cranky mother-in-law to a leaky roof to a 1957 Chevy! But that is not what the word *cross* meant to Jesus' first-century audience. It did not call to their minds the idea of long-term difficulties or troublesome burdens. It did not even evoke thoughts of Calvary—the Lord had not gone to the cross yet, and they did not understand that He would.

When Jesus said "take up your cross" to them, they thought of a cruel instrument of torture and death. They thought of dying in the most agonizing method known to man. They thought of poor, condemned criminals hanging on crosses by the roadside. Doubtless they had seen men executed in that fashion.

Jesus' listeners understood that He was calling them to die for Him. They knew He was asking them to make the ultimate sacrifice, to surrender to Him as Lord in every sense.

The Lord adds a final paradoxical thought on the meaning of discipleship: "He who has found his life will lose it, and he who has lost his life for My sake will find it" (Matt. 10:39). "He who has found his life" seems to refer to a person who has guarded his physical safety by denying Christ under pressure, or someone who clings to his life rather than taking up the cross. Because his first concern is securing his physical life, that person loses his eternal soul. Conversely, those who are willing to forfeit their lives for Christ's sake will receive eternal life.

The Bible does not teach salvation by martyrdom. The Lord was not advising the disciples to *try* to get themselves killed for Him. Again He was referring to a pattern, a direction. He was simply saying that genuine Christians do not shrink back, even in the face of death. To express it another way, when confronted with a decision between serving self and serving the Lord, the true disciple is the one who chooses to serve the Lord, even at great personal expense.

Again, this is not absolute in the sense that it disallows temporary failures like that of Peter. But even Peter *did* ultimately prove himself to be a true disciple, didn't he? The time came when he willingly gave His life for Jesus' sake.

Luke 9:23 records similar words of Jesus: "If anyone wishes to come after Me, he must deny himself, and take up his cross daily and follow Me." Notice the addition of the one word: "daily." The life of a disciple invites persecution and therefore must be a life of daily self-denial. Paul wrote to the Corinthians, "I affirm, brethren, by the boasting in you which I have in Christ Jesus our Lord, I die daily" (1 Cor. 15:31).

The idea of daily self-denial does not jibe with the contemporary supposition that believing in Jesus is a momentary decision. A true believer is one who signs up for life. The bumper sticker sentiment "Try Jesus" is a mentality foreign to real discipleship—faith is not an experiment, but a lifelong commitment. It means taking up the cross daily, giving all for Christ each day. It means no reservations, no uncertainty, no hesitation (Luke 9:59–61). It means nothing is knowingly held back, nothing purposely shielded from His lordship, nothing stubbornly kept from His control. It calls for a painful severing of ties with the world, a sealing of escape hatches, a ridding oneself of any kind of security to fall back on in case of failure. Genuine believers *know* they are going ahead with Christ until death.

Having put their hand to the plow, they will not look back (v. 62).

That is how it must be for all who would follow Jesus Christ. It is the stuff of true discipleship.

CHAPTER 11

The Cross

An obscure Hindu holy man named Rao flirted with worldwide fame in 1966. An eccentric, pompous mystic, Rao became convinced that he could walk on water. He was so confident in his own spiritual power that he announced he would perform the feat before a live audience. He sold tickets at a hundred dollars apiece. Bombay's elite turned out en masse to behold the spectacle.

The event was held in a large garden with a deep pool. A crowd of more than six hundred believers and curiosity-seekers assembled. The white-bearded yogi appeared in flowing robes and stepped confidently to the edge of the pool. He paused to pray silently. A reverent hush fell on the crowd. Rao opened his eyes, looked heavenward, and boldly stepped forward.

With an awkward splash he disappeared beneath the water.

Sputtering and red-faced, the holy man struggled to pull himself out of the water. Trembling with rage, he shook his finger at the silent, embarrassed crowd. "One of you," Rao bellowed indignantly, "is an unbeliever!"

A Show of Strength in Dying

All this world's so-called holy men contrast sharply with the One who really did walk on water. Jesus Christ performed many miracles, but He never staged them just for show. On the contrary, His greatest display of spiritual authority was when He died on a cross.

That is hard to comprehend but nevertheless true. Jesus did not fall victim to anyone or anything. He had come for the specific purpose of dying to atone for sin (Luke 19:10; John 1:29). His crucifixion was a vivid display of His authority over circumstances, men, and even death. Far from being a tragic end to His earthly ministry, it was the culmination of all He had set out to do.

That biblical truth, unfortunately, is often overlooked. People have for centuries argued about who was to blame for killing Jesus. Sadly, some have even used the issue to justify anti-Semitism, blaming the entire Jewish race for Jesus' death.

Certainly the Jewish leaders who condemned Him were culpable. They plotted, concocted false charges against Him, and blackmailed the Roman governor Pontius Pilate into carrying out their will. They were by no means innocent.

And the Roman government must share the guilt. Those who represented Rome in Jerusalem set aside justice to appease an angry crowd. They executed an innocent man.

But Jesus was not ultimately a victim of either Rome or the Jewish leaders. The apostle Peter says in Acts 2:23 that Jesus was "delivered over by the predetermined plan and foreknowledge of God." The Jewish leaders and the Roman officials who carried out His crucifixion undeniably bear guilt for the sin of what they did, but God Himself had foreordained how Jesus would die.

Thus Jesus' death was an act of the Son's submissive obedience to the Father's will. And Jesus Himself was in absolute control. He said,

"I lay down My life that I may take it again. No one has taken it away from Me, but I lay it down on My own initiative. I have authority to lay it down, and I have authority to take it up again. This commandment I received from My Father" (John 10:17–18).

Do not think for a moment that anyone could kill Jesus against His will. The divine plan could never be short-circuited by human or satanic plots. Jesus even told Pilate, "You would have no authority over Me, unless it had been given you from above" (John 19:11). Mobs tried to murder Jesus. They once sought to hurl Him off a cliff (Luke 4:29–30) and repeatedly attempted to stone Him (John 8:59; 10:31). Again and again He simply passed through their midst because His time had not yet come (cf. John 7:30; 8:20).

When the hour of His death finally did come, Jesus knew it (Matt. 26:18). Fully comprehending all it would entail in terms of the pain and agony of bearing the sin of the world, He nevertheless submitted Himself willingly. John 18:4 tells us that when the soldiers came to arrest Him in the Garden of Gethsemane, "Jesus, *knowing all the things that were coming upon Him*, went forth, and said to them, 'Whom do you seek?'" He willingly surrendered Himself to them. It was His hour now, the time foreordained by God.

Control over Every Detail

No passage of Scripture speaks with more force about Jesus' omnipotence in the midst of His agony on the cross than John 19:28–30: "Jesus, knowing that all things had already been accomplished, to fulfill the Scripture, said, 'I am thirsty.' A jar full of sour wine was standing there; so they put a sponge full of the sour wine upon a branch of hyssop and brought it up to His mouth. Therefore when Jesus had received the sour wine, He said, 'It is finished!' And He bowed His head and gave up His spirit."

Throughout the crucifixion, Jesus Christ was on a divine timetable. God was sovereignly directing every incident. Step by step, each detail of Old Testament prophecy was fulfilled. Psalm 22 and Isaiah 53 in particular outlined prophetically the specific features of His death. All of them were carried out precisely.

As He hung on the cross, Jesus knew that "all things had already been accomplished" (John

19:28)—all, that is, but one final prophecy. Psalm 69:21, where Christ speaks prophetically of His own death, says, "For my thirst they gave me vinegar to drink." And so "to fulfill the Scripture, [He] said, 'I am thirsty'" (John 19:28). The soldiers responded. They were under divine impetus; God was moving to fulfill the prophecy.

Some have maintained that Jesus was simply a man who purposely engineered details of His life and death to coincide with selected Old Testament prophecies. A well-known book of the 1960s made precisely that argument. The author pointed to phrases like "to fulfill the Scripture" (John 19:28) as proof that Jesus manipulated circumstances to give the appearance of fulfilling Scripture.

But a mere man trying to mislead people could not have had the kind of sovereign control over events Jesus repeatedly displayed. This verse proves why. It was not Jesus alone, but everyone around Him—His enemies included—who fulfilled precisely the details of Old Testament prophecy: "A jar full of sour wine [vinegar] was standing there; so they put a sponge full of the sour wine upon a branch of hyssop and brought it up to His mouth" (John 19:29). Exactly as the prophecy had predicted.

Note that the sponge was lifted to His mouth on a branch of hyssop. Hyssop, a long reed with a bushy end, had a history of significance in the Jewish sacrificial system. Exodus 12:22 prescribed hyssop as the tool by which lamb's blood was to be applied to the doorposts and lintel during the first Passover. Hyssop was used in many of the Levitical sacrifices (Lev. 14:4, 6, 49–52; Num. 19:6, 18). It was so closely tied to sacrifices for sin that when David wrote his great psalm of penitence, he said, "Purify me with hyssop, and I shall be clean" (Ps. 51:7).

How fitting, then, that hyssop should be the tool at the sacrifice of the true Passover Lamb! Do you think the Roman soldiers understood the relevance of what they were doing? I am certain they did not. But Jesus sovereignly saw to it that they carried out every detail, although they surely thought *they* were displaying their power over *Him*!

It Is Finished!

John 19:30 says, "Therefore when Jesus had received the sour wine, He said, 'It is finished!'" The Greek expression is only one word—*tetelestai*. It was not the groan or curse of a victim; it was the proclamation of a victor. It was a shout of triumph: "IT IS FINISHED!"

The wealth of meaning in that phrase is surely impossible for the human mind to fathom. What was finished? His earthly life? Yes, but far more. Every detail of redemptive prophecy? Certainly, but not that alone.

The work of redemption was done. All that the law of God required, full atonement for sins, everything the symbolism of ceremonial law foreshadowed—the work that the Father had given Him to do—everything was done. Nothing was left. The ransom was paid. The wages of sin were settled. Divine justice was satisfied. The work of Christ was thus accomplished in toto. The Lamb of God had taken away the sins of the world (John 1:29). There was nothing more on earth for Him to do except die so that He might rise again.

Here it is appropriate to add a crucial footnote: when Jesus said, "It is finished," He meant it. Nothing can be added to what He did. Many people believe they must supplement His work with good deeds of their own. They believe they must facilitate their own redemption through baptism, other sacraments and religious rituals, benevolent deeds, or whatever else they can accomplish through their own efforts. But no works of human righteousness can expand on what Jesus accomplished for us. "He saved us, not on the basis of deeds which we have done in righteousness, but according to His mercy" (Titus 3:5). The beginning and the end of our salvation was consummated by Jesus Christ, and we can contribute nothing.

What would you think if I took a pen and tried to add more features to the Mona Lisa? What if I got a hammer and chisel and offered to refine Michelangelo's Moses? That would be a travesty. They are masterpieces! No one needs to add to them.

In an infinitely greater way, that is true of Jesus' atoning work. He has paid the full price of our sins. He has purchased our redemption. He offers a salvation from sin that is complete in every sense. "It is finished!" Nothing we can do would in any way add to what He accomplished on our behalf.

Having finished His work, our Lord "bowed His head and gave up His spirit" (John 19:30). There was no jerk, no sudden slump. He bowed His head. The Greek word evokes the picture of gently placing one's head on a pillow. In the

171

truest sense, no man took Jesus' life from Him. He laid it down of His own accord (cf. John 10:17–18). He simply and quietly yielded up His spirit, commending Himself into the Father's hands (Luke 23:46).

Only the omnipotent God who is Lord of all could do that. Death could not claim Jesus apart from His own will. He died in complete control of all that was happening to Him. Even in His death He was Lord.

To the human eye Jesus looked like a pathetic casualty, powerless in the hands of mighty men. But the opposite was true. He was the One in charge. He proved it a few days later by forever bursting the bonds of death when He rose from the grave (1 Cor. 15:20–57).

And He is still in charge. "For to this end Christ died and lived again, that He might be Lord both of the dead and of the living" (Rom. 14:9).

This, then, is the gospel our Lord sends us forth to proclaim: that Jesus Christ, who is God incarnate, humbled Himself to die on our behalf. Thus He became the sinless sacrifice to pay the penalty of our guilt. He rose from the dead to declare with power that He is Lord over all, and He offers eternal life freely to sinners

who will surrender to Him in humble, repentant faith. This gospel promises nothing to the
haughty rebel, but for broken, penitent sinners, it
graciously offers everything that pertains to life
and godliness (2 Peter 1:3).